Why Your Business Must Have Cybersecurity Risk Assessments

Learn the Reasons WHY
From 14 Cybersecurity Experts

Published by Prominence Publishing,
www.prominencepublishing.com.

Why Your Business Must Have Cybersecurity Risk Assessments -- 1st ed.

ISBN: 978-1-988925-91-2

Contents

Foreword

By Chris Wiser...1

3 Types of Cyber Security Breaches & How Your Business Can Avoid Becoming a Victim

By Jim Reichard..3

How Your Business Can Avoid the Next Cyber Attack

By Michael Allen Beck 11

Is Your Business Risking It All?

By Brian Artigas..21

Three Security Measures Your Business Needs Now

By Christopher Bartosz 39

The Truth About How Hackers Exploit Your Business

By Chuck Dornon 47

Security 101: What Can You Do to Protect Your Business from the Unknown?

By Mike Bloomfield 59

Will My Business be the Next Target for Hackers?

By Shulem Moskovits..71

Cyber Security Deep Dive: Are Your Employees The Weakest Link?

By Brett Gallant...81

Three Ways to Prevent Getting Hacked

By Andrew Baker..99

Protecting Your Business - Learn the Steps to Reducing Your Risk

By Peter Zendzian..117

Six Reasons Why Your Business Should Conduct Regular Security Assessments

By Joseph Salazar..129

Three Types of Cyber Security Breaches & How Your Business Can Minimize Risk

By Gregory Bledsoe 143

Why Your Disaster Recovery Plan Could Save Your Business

By David Burton and Wes Jensen 151

Reduce Your Liability & Identify Your Business Risk

By John Hill 169

Foreword

By Chris Wiser

Most business owners understand what cybersecurity "is" but never quite understand the need for "it" in their businesses. Most of the time, Information Technology is thought of more as an expense than a necessity, which is why most business owners continue to look the other way when it comes to implementing a strong cybersecurity plan for their business.

Cybercrime affects all businesses, regardless of size or location, and as technology advances and we continue to live in a remote, digital world, it is crucial to understand the NEED for Cybersecurity. The fact of the matter is that business owners who are not protecting their business data, their assets and their employees are at great risk.

It is not a surprise that cybersecurity should be a crucial part of every business, as we have seen a huge increase in cybercrime over the course of the past couple of years. Understanding the risks and vulnerabilities present within your business is crucial in protecting your business assets and safeguarding your data. During the past few years, cybersecurity experts have found methods to mitigate cyberattacks;

however it is important to first understand what those risks are to implement a strong cybersecurity plan that will protect your business from cybercrime.

The best method to determine your business risks and vulnerabilities is to have a Cybersecurity Risk Assessment completed for your business. This assessment will help you determine exactly what risks your business has, the effect(s) of those risk(s) and how to mitigate those risks from dismantling your business from the inside out.

Cybersecurity is not a commodity; rather, it is a necessity for every business owner, and it is important to spread awareness throughout our business community. In this book, we have brought together fourteen cybersecurity experts to help business owners understand WHY cybersecurity is crucial and WHY every business must have a cybersecurity assessment completed; and further, what needs to be done to start protecting your business data and assets from cybercriminals.

Chris Wiser,

CEO, 7 Figure MSP

Speaker/Trainer/
Entrepreneur Coach

Three Types of Cyber Security Breaches & How Your Business Can Avoid Becoming a Victim

By Jim Reichard

Today's cyber space is full of things. Thus, the acronym "IoT" (Internet of Things). Our lives are filled with devices. The watch on our wrists, the phone in our pockets, the smart bed we got out of this morning that tells us how we slept last night, the smart coffee pot that turned itself on, the smart garage doors that we open when leaving the house that triggered the smart thermostats to adjust, the smart lights to turn off and the smart cameras to record the motion of us leaving our homes. Oh, and Alexa and Siri are also listening.

All these things can be a potential threat to security. This entire threat surface must be protected. Although the vendors for most of these products do a fair job keeping them secure, all these devices can be compromised, and we haven't even arrived at the office yet!

Things We Are Finding Every Day in Today's Cyber Workspaces

$250,000 vanishes in minutes.

A company in a state of panic and dismay states that something strange has happened to them. Their CFO had received an email from the CEO saying to transfer a large amount of funds to a new bank account that they would be using from now on. It came from the president of the company and looked legit, so they proceeded to make the transfer.

What happened?

An attacker used an email phishing attack to gather credentials to a user's email account. They then carried out a man-in-the-middle attack by using social engineering to learn the behaviors and mannerisms of the people they intended to attack. They waited in the system for six months and watched. They learned the employees' habits and waited for the right moment to strike. Then, Payday.

What could have been done differently?

Training the users with cyber security awareness training and fake phishing attempts that when triggered, force mandatory training will help users understand when they are being phished. Monitoring of login attempts and multi-factor authentication could have prevented this.

HIPAA Wall of Shame!

A physician's office gets a call from a patient stating that their information has been found on the dark web and compromised. This doctor's office is the only one the patient has been to in ten years. The office has an audit done and discovers that one of their outdated servers has not only been compromised but a data breach has occurred. They are now in clear violation of HIPAA and must notify all their patients of the breach. The remediation costs hundreds of thousands of dollars. The local authorities are involved, the office becomes a crime scene, and they end up on the HIPAA wall of shame. (Yes... that's a real thing.)

What happened?

An old, outdated web server was compromised, and an attacker used it to infiltrate the network, gain access to, and export patient data to the dark web for sale via an accessible SQL database.

What could have been done differently?

This could have been prevented by securing the network properly, keeping the server up-to-date, retiring it, or removing it from the network.

$527,000 machinery payment, gone.

A call from a frantic CFO stating that they called their customer about a missing payment. The customer states that they paid the invoice to the new account as directed, then produces an email from that very CFO that told the customer to make their normal ACH payment to a new account.

What happened?

Another phishing attack where the attacker gained access to email, then carried out a man-in-the-middle attack to intercept payments to the company.

What could have been done differently?

Putting in place change policies that require two people to sign off on financial changes and monitoring user logins could have prevented this. When audited, there were login attempts from the CFO in two different places at the same time and no change policies in place.

BUSINESS DOWN 4 DAYS!

A distress call from a prospective client who is in desperate need of help. Their whole business is down, all their files, servers, and backups have been encrypted and held for ransom. Pay the demanded $150,000 ransom? The attacker won't return their emails, and it's been four days!

What happened?

The client unknowingly had ports open to the internet from their firewall allowing an attacker to brute force attack their simple password and gain access to the servers and deploy ransomware.

What could have been done differently?

If audited, this could have been prevented. Keeping insecure ports closed is essential to the security of the network. Strong password policies need to be enforced. Changing passwords every 90 days is no longer recommended. It creates predictable passwords. Use a strong pass phrase instead of a word. Keeping backups protected and offsite is also a must.

***

These are the many forms of attacks that happen daily across the globe.

With proper protections and training, we can disrupt this increasing trend of cyber crime.

You say to yourself, "Self, I have good IT support, they're doing all the things to protect me, right?" (Probably not. Ask them.)

Ask yourself, "Self, how do I know for sure that I'm protected? Am I qualified to know if my team is keeping me safe? Do I study cyber security and know how to protect my organization from the daily changing threats?"

Here at AllTech IT Solutions, we do. We help hundreds of companies nationwide protect their businesses against growing threats. We are constantly training and evolving to combat cyber crime.

"But I like my IT company or team," you say. That's great, we can make them better with our co-managed solutions. Let us help them help you.

About the Author

Jim Reichard is the president of Alltech IT Solutions, founded in 2004. He graduated from the UAB School of Engineering in Advanced Networking in 2001 and has been continuing his education ever since. He is an experienced corporate officer with a demonstrated history in the information technology and services industry. He is highly skilled in cyber security, advanced networking, infrastructure, virtualization, and managed services.

He believes that customer service and his client's success through technology is paramount.

Call to schedule a comprehensive cyber security risk assessment!

205-290-0215 or sales@alltechsupport.com

How Your Business Can Avoid the Next Cyber Attack

By Michael Allen Beck

The Boy Scout motto, "Be Prepared" means to always be alert and at a state of readiness. We prepare for many things in our life. We prepare for the birth of a child. We prepare for accidents by buying insurance. In California, we prepare for earthquakes by having spare clothes, water, and food in our earthquake kits. In the South, when we are told that a hurricane is coming, what do we do? We prepare. Being prepared does not mean that the impending disaster won't cause us damage; instead, we do what we can to minimize its impact, to make sure we can recover as gracefully as possible. This same need to prepare exists in our businesses. What if the worst happens? What if we are hit with a cyber attack that takes down our computer network? What if we can't get to our data, or our accounting systems? Who do we owe money to? Or the bigger issue, who owes us money? What if your payroll account was compromised and emptied out? What if your email system was not accessible or was wiped out? These issues are devastating to a business. How long can you survive without your data? One week, one month? What if you never get it back at all? Will your business survive? According to Fundara, 60% of small businesses that suffer a cyber attack go out of business within 6 months. [1]

This does not have to be the case. There are things we can do to mitigate these effects and recover gracefully with little to no interruption to our business. It all starts with knowing your risk. It all starts with a cyber risk assessment.

***

A financial services firm has been growing steadily for years, doing great and becoming very profitable. They started with just dad and his two sons in a small office in Newport Beach, California. They kept their clients' portfolios growing, even during big downturns in the market. When they started the business in the mid 90s, technology was their advantage. They had great internet access for the times and even utilized remote access so they could have access from home. As they grew and added staff, they continued to invest in their systems. Over the years, the network, servers, and computers have been upgraded, changed, and reconfigured. Business was good and their people were efficient. One of the sons is tech savvy and can

---

[1] https://www.fundera.com/resources/small-business-cyber-security-statistics

perform basic IT troubleshooting. To save on some costs, he does much of the day-to-day IT work himself. This was a client that upgraded regularly and followed all the recommendations from their support company. Cyber threats were not really a thing back then. IT support companies mainly worried about computer viruses and hardware failures. The financial services company put in best-of-breed antivirus and a good backup system.

Fast forward to 2015. The business is thriving and has grown to 20 employees. Just like any other company, staff members have left and new staff have come onboard. The tech savvy son has moved on as well. Many of the staff have a PC in the office and a laptop for mobility. They remote into the system when working away from the office. The method for remote access has evolved over the years and the configuration of the firewall has changed to match. Here is the danger. As things change, IT adds in the changes. Many times, IT does not clean up the previous settings. This is called "IT sprawl."

The financial services company pays for break/fix support. When something breaks, they call IT to get it fixed. When a new employee starts, they call IT to get them setup. In this scenario, the IT support company usually is not aware of all the things that have transpired before in the company's systems. They only get a small glimpse during the times when the company calls for support. The IT company in a break/fix model rarely has the chance to do housekeeping to rid the system of old configurations and settings that are no longer used or needed. They are only called and authorized to fix issues as they arise. In addition, there have been at least five different IT companies supporting this system over the years, with no documentation of the network and what changes have been made.

In November of 2018, all was running well. The client had not needed to call support at all for over a month. It's Thanksgiving week and the phones are quiet as the company plans to be closed for four days over the holiday. That Friday night, bad actors hit. They had noticed that the firewall had open RDP ports ready to be attacked. Come Monday morning, all the computers were up and on, but no one could access any files. On their screens was a note explaining that all their data had been encrypted and that they must pay a ransom to get it back.

My company, NetMinded, was called that Monday morning after the holiday at 6:00am by a frantic office manager explaining the situation. We responded. The client, to save some money, had been backing up to a network storage appliance instead of having a managed offsite backup solution. The ransomware got to that device as well. There was no clear path to recovery. It was not easy, but we eventually were able to get them up and running, but not without significant pain and interruption. The issue is without good, tested, protected backups, we had to rebuild each computer and server from the ground up. It took two weeks just to get the basics going, and well over a month to smooth out all the issues. Thank goodness the accountant had a copy of the QuickBooks file, and there was an external hard drive that had all the server data as of six months ago. Unfortunately, the MS Exchange server was a total loss. We were not able to recover any email at all.

On that Monday, we called the local police department and filed a report (for insurance mainly), then called the FBI and the SEC. The company had insurance with a cyber clause, so we called them, too. They immediately took action and sent down a forensics team to image all the PCs and servers to preserve evidence and see if they could break the encryption (which they could not). The company had to report, by law, to all their clients that they had been compromised and offer their clients credit protection. This was devastating. The phone rang nonstop for months, with clients asking if their money was safe, if their identities were going to be stolen and used. Many clients left. There was no telling what kind of impact this was going to have long term. The financial services company survived, but just barely.

With any new client, my firm starts with doing a risk assessment to discover vulnerabilities, misconfigurations, unused/old settings, and login accounts that may exist. This discovery is critical so we can find the holes that need to be plugged and where a network is vulnerable. In some cases, we have discovered that the prospect has already been breached and that an ongoing attack is happening. Computer systems are only as secure as the least secure computer/endpoint is. Many times, we find one or two old systems with an outdated operating system still online, because the client needs to access an old software program that only works on the old system. These vulnerabilities, if exploited, can kill any business. Once discovered, there are measures that we can take to isolate the old systems and allow them to operate safely. We just need to know that they are there.

***

If the financial services company had done a cyber risk assessment, they would have known that the open RDP ports used for remote access years ago were still there. They would be closed, and this attack would never have happened.

After the fact, the need to know your vulnerabilities seems obvious, but most businesses don't do a risk assessment, and even more disturbing, most small business IT support companies don't push for them. Since COVID, cyber attacks are on the rise at a level never seen before. Insurance companies have had record numbers of claims due to cyber events and record payouts. This is forcing them to change how they operate and how they evaluate their clients' claims. The industry has now started using "gross negligence" clauses. If a policyholder does not maintain their systems up to *industry standards* and follow *best practices* in an attempt to provide *meaningful safeguards* against an attack, the insurance carrier will deny the claim. They are now looking for ways not to pay claims. They are shifting responsibility to the end client and their IT provider.

Cyber risk assessments are now asked for during the application for a new policy, and for the renewal of an existing policy. They are no longer optional. Companies can no longer ignore their own responsibility to know the state of their systems. Not taking preventative steps will cause claims to go unpaid and could likely cause your business to fail. Legislation is in the works that would hold corporate officers accountable for the state of their computer systems. There is also legislation in the works that will mandate IT support companies to formally inform any client or potential client of their risks and the steps needed to help mitigate those risks.

Recently, a very reputable manufacturing company was asked by a large potential new client for the results of their most recent cyber risk assessment. Fortunately, they had it, and it was recent, allowing them to bid on the new business and secure a contract. This is now becoming commonplace. Companies are concerned that their suppliers and vendors could be ignoring their vulnerabilities and looking at how that may affect them when a cyber event happens.

Cyber events will happen. There is a new cyber attack happening every 39 seconds. Cyber crime is a six trillion-dollar industry. It cannot be stopped. Cyber criminals will not go away. This is the new normal.

What we *can* do is put in place tools and policies that allow us to detect and mitigate these events, greatly reducing or even eliminating any interruption to our business. A cyber risk assessment is the first and most important step to make sure your business is ready, and that your company is cyber resilient.

Ask my team at NetMinded how to get started. Let us show you how this critical step is also the easiest. If you tell our team that you read this chapter, we will give you 20% off your risk assessment.

Contact us at becybersafe@netminded.com or call us at 800-909-3819. You can also visit our website at: www.NetMinded.com/HowYourBusinessCanAvoidTh eNextCyberAttack

About the Author

 Michael Allen Beck is a leading cyber security expert in Orange County, California. For over two decades, Michael has managed cyber security and network infrastructures for small businesses in a wide variety of industries. Starting in the late 90's, Michael Beck saw the need for high level skill sets to manage IT and propel small business growth with a competitive edge.

As an Adjunct professor with UCLA Extension, Cal Poly Pomona, and Computer Learning Centers, he developed curriculum and taught Microsoft Systems Engineering courses (MCSE), CompTIA courses, and Cisco networking courses achieving the highest rated student certification rates. In an effort to provide work experience for young adults entering the industry, he hired his best students to work with his company, NetMinded, to service the SMB market.

Through the years Michael has stayed at the cutting edge of the industry. He has been a member of the FBI Infragard and is currently a member of the Orange County Sheriff Department PSR, High-Tech Services Reserve Squad (HTSRS), Investigative Support Reserve Unit (ISRU). Michael has also served on his local

Community College technology advisory board. His 26 years of experience in an ever changing high-tech environment has given Michael vision of where SMB technology is going. His insights and methodology for arming small businesses to defend against cyber threats reflect his commitment to helping entre- preneurs manage their risk.

Michael lives in Irvine, California with his wife, triplets... and a delightful Shih-Tzu named Coco.

Is Your Business Risking It All?

By Brian Artigas

"Everyone has a plan 'til they get punched in the mouth."

-Mike Tyson

While Mike Tyson wasn't referring to cyber security when he made that statement, it has a certain universal wisdom to it. I can't say for sure what the likelihood is that a person will get punched in the mouth as a result of being the victim of a cyber security attack, but I'm fairly certain that they'll wish it was the only consequence.

CNBC's Momentiv Q3 2021 "Small Business Survey"[2] found that 59% of small business owners feel confident that they can quickly resolve any cyber attack, but only 28% of them said they have an actual plan in place to

---

[2] https://www.cnbc.com/2021/08/10/main-street-overconfidence-small-businesses-dont-worry-about-hacking.html

respond to a cyber attack. The worst time to figure out how to respond to a crisis is while it's happening.

What is the likelihood of a cyber attack?

In March of 2020, the international law firm, ReedSmith[3] stated, "Scams have increased by 400% over the last month. Criminals seem to be taking full advantage of a time of crisis [referring to COVID-19], targeting not just individuals and a vulnerable population, but also organizations."

In Verizon's "2019 Data Breach Investigations Report"[4] it was found that 43% of cyber attacks involved small businesses. The same report stated that 59% of breaches took months or longer to discover. That last statistic is the scariest because a considerable amount of damage can be done over the course of several months. The 2020 SolarWinds Orion attack is a perfect example.

In 2020 there was an attack on SolarWinds' Orion IT monitoring and management software platform. It all began in September 2019 when threat actors gained unauthorized access to the SolarWinds network. Then in February of 2020, the threat actors injected some malware, called Sunburst, into the Orion software. Then in March of 2020, SolarWinds unknowingly sent

---

[3] https://www.reedsmith.com/en/perspectives/2020/03/corona virus-is-now-possibly-the-largest-ever-security-threat
[4] https://enterprise.verizon.com/resources/reports/2019-data-breach-investigations-report.pdf

out Orion software updates that were infected with the Sunburst malware. Of SolarWinds' 300,000 clients, more than 18,000 of them were unwittingly infected with the Sunburst malware, until it was discovered and reported in December of 2020. One can imagine how much data was breached in the nine months these threat actors had access to these 18,000 clients' systems.

This leads to a few questions that I ask you, the reader, to ask yourself:

- Have you ever been hacked before?

- How would you know if you have been hacked?

- What would you do if you sat down in front of your computer right now and found that all your data was inaccessible?

- What would you do if you logged into your bank account and discovered that all of your money was gone?

- If you had to notify your customers that all of the data you had on them (contact info, credit card or banking information, etc.) had been leaked and had fallen into the hands of hackers, how would that conversation go?

- What have you done to prevent and plan for a cyber attack?

The above questions are going to make some folks a little uncomfortable because they might not be able to answer them. Or if they are answering the questions honestly, the answers may not be what they want. That's ok. The first step in solving a problem is realizing there is one.

Have you been hacked before?

The fact is, there have been billions of records breached that you have virtually no control over whatsoever. Facebook, Marriott, Microsoft, Canva, T-Mobile, Twitter Yahoo, LinkedIn, MySpace, Twitch, and so many others, have had massive data breaches[5] in the last five years. The likelihood that your information is in one of those breaches is high.

When these breaches take place, the data is often sold on the dark web for other hackers to purchase and exploit. When we run dark web scans for clients' email addresses and passwords, it's not uncommon to find credentials that are actively being used on more than one service or account. It's very possible that your data may be floating around on the dark web for someone to purchase and use against you. The best way to prevent this from happening is to use a password manager (secured by a strong password and two-factor authentication) to create and store strong passwords for all your online services and accounts. Each account or service should have its own unique password.

---

[5] https://www.informationisbeautiful.net/visualizations/worlds-biggest-data-breaches-hacks

As of this writing, the two most common cyber attacks are malware and phishing. A phishing attack is most often the way malware gets on a computer in the first place.

Phishing is when someone sends an email falsely claiming to be a legitimate person or organization. The purpose of this email is to trick the recipient into opening an infected attachment, sending some sort of critical information such as email or banking credentials that can be used to benefit the attacker or even trick the victim into sending the attacker money.

Malware is any software designed with a malicious intent such as spying on the activities on your computer, remotely controlling your computer, or controlling the data on your computer, among other use cases. The most common malware is ransomware, which makes all the data on your computer inaccessible by encrypting it and then demanding a ransom to provide the decryption key to make the data accessible again. Ransomware malware usually spreads very quickly if prevention methods haven't been employed.

Town of Jupiter, Florida Ransomware Attacks

In December of 2018, in my hometown of Jupiter, FL, the Town of Jupiter was the victim of a ransomware attack. The attack was a result of a phishing email that pretended to be an invoice from the shipping company, DHL. In this case, one person opened the infected attachment in the phishing email and it infected a large portion of their network, crippling many of the town's electronically-controlled functions. Thankfully, the Town had good backups, and they had most of the critical systems back online within 48 hours without paying the ransom.

In March of 2020, the Town fell victim to yet another ransomware attack. This time it took three weeks to get all systems back online. Thankfully, again, the Town had good backups, so they didn't pay the ransom.

How would YOU know if you were hacked?

If someone had compromised your systems and was quietly exfiltrating data, or using your systems as part of a network of other computers, known as a botnet, to attack other systems, how would you know? Do you have any alerting method in place beyond basic antivirus and/or firewalls? Are you alerted when there are multiple incorrect logon attempts? When several files on your network are modified or deleted at the same time? Or when an administrative user logs into a system?

Attackers gain access to systems through many ways, the most common of which are malware and social engineering. Social engineering is when an attacker scams a victim by contacting them and tricking them into giving the attacker some sort of access or critical information. When an attacker manages to get access to a system, they will typically attempt to install a utility called a RAT (remote access tool), that will allow them persistent access, meaning if they get disconnected, they can get back in. This is called "establishing a foothold." Once a foothold has been established, it's not uncommon for attackers to download data from the victim's computer network. In many cases, if the attacker finds backup software on the system, they'll disable it and attempt to delete the backups. If there's no logging and alerting in place on a network, they can do this silently without anyone noticing. Once they've gotten everything from the system they want or need, they can then run a ransomware attack on it, and the victim will have no choice but to pay the ransom because their backups have been deleted.

What would you do if you sat down in front of your computer right now and found that all of your data was inaccessible?

It's Monday morning, and you walk into your office and sit down at your workstation, only to find a message on your screen that says:

"YOUR COMPUTER HAS BEEN INFECTED, YOU HAVE 6 DAYS TO SEND US 5 BITCOIN TO GET ACCESS TO YOUR FILES, AFTER 6 DAYS THE PRICE GOES UP TO 7.5 BITCOIN."

Nothing you try will allow you to have access to your files. You get up and go to another computer, only to find the same message. What's your next step? Do you have a plan?

What would you do if you logged into your bank account and discovered that all of your money was gone?

I often get surprised looks from folks when I tell them that the FDIC does not insure your bank accounts against theft or fraud. If a hacker gets your banking information and transfers your money out of your account to an offshore account, the FDIC will not cover that, and the bank, in most cases, cannot do anything to reverse it.

Scammers are getting clever

My team came across a scam not too long ago where the attacker was able to obtain a victim's online credit card account credentials. This account was protected with two-factor authentication (2FA). In this case, when one tries to log in, it will send a text message to the account owner's mobile phone with a code that they must type in to finish logging in. The attacker called the victim on the phone at around midnight when the victim was asleep. The attacker stated that they were from the credit card company and the victim's credit card was stolen. This naturally disturbed the half-asleep victim and caused them to panic. The attacker, posing as an employee of the credit card company, then stated that in order to verify they were speaking with the right person, they would send them a text message with a code that they would need to read back. The attacker in this case was attaching the victim's credit card to an Apple Pay account, which requires one to log into the credit card company's site to approve the Apple Pay service for use of the card. The victim read back the 2FA code to the attacker and the attacker was able to add the account to their Apple Pay service (which was likely also stolen from another victim). The victim contacted us for advice, and we advised they call their credit card company immediately. They reported back that they called, and the credit card company confirmed that they were scammed.

Thankfully, banks can reverse most credit card transactions. But in most cases, banks cannot reverse ATM and ACH debit transactions or wire transfers. If an attacker gets the credentials to your bank account, you have a real problem on your hands. They could drain the account and you would have little to no recourse.

If you had to notify your customers and employees that all of the data you had on them had been leaked and it had fallen into the hands of hackers, how would that conversation go?

Depending on the nature of your business, the greatest source of risk in your company is likely the data you store. If you're a medical office, you're storing Protected Health Information (PHI), however most other businesses are storing Personally Identifiable Information (PII). If your company writes payroll, you have W4 and W9 forms, and you may have direct deposit forms with your employees' ACH information. If your business provides health insurance or life insurance, you may have some PHI if you store the applications. What do you store about your clients? It's likely you'll have, at the very least, their name, address, phone number, and email address. That's enough to launch a phishing attack. Do you have their credit card or ACH information? Do you have any personal information on them such as birthdays, family members' names, pets' names, etc.? With that information an attacker may have answers to security questions used to reset passwords. Also, when an attacker attempts to scam a victim, the more information they can reference from the victim, the more likely they are to succeed.

Many states have data privacy laws that require businesses to exercise due care in protecting the PII in their custody. I'm not an attorney or an expert on data privacy laws outside the federal level and Florida, but I can state that all the laws I've reviewed have some sort of notification requirement. Upon a breach, you're required to notify people whose data was involved in the breach. The question remains, how would you broach that subject with your clients? What sort of consequences might there be regarding your clients' trust in you and your business? Once your breach has been publicized, how might you win the trust of future prospects? Might you have to worry about lawsuits?

What can you do about all of this risk?

The first step is to complete a risk assessment on your company to determine what exactly is at risk. I highly recommend you work with a professional to accomplish this. Someone who does this everyday will have the training and experience to spot risks where you may not realize they exist. They can also provide you with cost effective strategies to address their findings.

There are four ways to approach cyber security risks:

- Risk Acceptance

- Risk Avoidance

- Risk Mitigation

- Risk Transfer

Risk Acceptance

There may be some risks of which potential impact would be negligible or the cost to mitigate them outweighs the benefit. In these cases, it's recommended that you document the risk, noting that you're accepting it and why.

You'll want to review your risk strategy on a regular basis. I recommend annually at a minimum, but quarterly or even monthly would be ideal, depending on the nature of your business. During your risk strategy review, you'll want to review your accepted risks to determine whether they have remained the same; has the cost to mitigate come down to a level where it's worth mitigating, or has the risk become a big enough issue to do something about it?

Risk Avoidance

You may be using cloud software that provides convenience but your risk assessment shows that the company would experience significant loss if the cloud solution was compromised. In this case, it may be in the company's best interest to give up the convenience to avoid the risk altogether.

We often see this with free, cloud storage solutions. Some businesses will use a free, cloud storage service to store some data out of convenience. When we advise them that the free version provides no guarantee of security, they may decide that the convenience is not worth the risk and stop using the solution. It's worth noting that paid-for services often have a security guarantee, but make sure you get that guarantee in writing and that the service meets any regulatory requirements you must adhere to.

Risk Mitigation

I often tell people that cyber security risk mitigation is accomplished in layers, like an onion. If you look at most banks or casinos, they have locks on the doors, burglar alarms, security cameras, and security guards. Some have even more sophisticated systems when you get closer to the vault. If you've ever seen the movie Ocean's Eleven, you know what I'm talking about.

As it pertains to cyber security, qualified cyber security professionals will stack systems and services to get what they feel is the best mitigation strategy for a company. These often include:

- Signature-based antimalware software
- Artificial intelligence-based endpoint detection and response software
- Unified threat management firewall
- Server and workstation activity monitoring and alerting
- Application whitelisting
- DNS filtering
- Multi-factor authentication for remote access
- Multi-factor authentication for privileged access
- and the list goes on

Most of these services are much less effective if they aren't being actively monitored. If a system alerts on a threat and nobody is there to see the alert, what good does the system do? Some systems will proactively quarantine the system, others will not. It depends on the system and how it's configured.

Risk Transfer

It's always recommended that any business using any sort of computer equipment have cyber liability insurance. A cyber liability policy allows you to transfer risk to the insurance company. Important to note: Read your policy for exclusions and terms such as "gross negligence," "failure to maintain," and "due care." With so many breaches happening lately, the attorneys at these insurance companies have been busy trying to mitigate *their* risk. They want to make sure you're taking the necessary steps to exercise "due care" and take "commercially reasonable measures" to mitigating your risk.

Security Awareness Training

Human error is the #1 cyber security threat to business. Providing your employees (and participating yourself) with security awareness training is one of the most effective risk mitigation actions you can take — on top of the standard mitigation measures to secure the network, of course. This training should consist of annual training with a test to make sure employees understand and have retained the information. There's no point in providing the training if someone is going to sit through it, scrolling through social media, ignoring the material. Then, it is recommended that you have regular weekly or monthly reminders to keep security top-of-mind and post reminders around the workplace.

PLAN, PLAN, PLAN

In cyber security, the saying rings true, "a failure to plan is a plan to fail." It is vital for your business to have a plan in place for disaster recovery. Use your security risk assessment to determine how many ways your critical systems can be taken offline, and put together a plan with your IT team or IT provider to deal with calamity when it hits. Make sure you test your plan to make sure it actually works. What good is a backup if it doesn't work, or doesn't have all of the critical data when you restore it?

Hackers are rarely just some guys in black hoodies in a basement somewhere. They're big businesses now, and some are state-owned. They have human resources, support staff, development staff, and marketing staff, just like many modern businesses. They make their living by exploiting people and their businesses.

I hope I've been able to illustrate why it's imperative to take cyber security seriously and address your risk. My company, Allstate Computers, is a cyber security-focused IT service provider. If we can be of assistance, please reach out and we'll be happy to help. If you have an existing IT service provider or IT department, contact them and make sure you and they are addressing your risk.

About the Author

Brian Artigas began tinkering with computers as a child living in Vero Beach, FL. in the 1980's. His love for computers and technology landed him his first job building and repairing computers at a small, local computer store in 1997. In 2001, he started a web hosting company called Netrodyne Interactive Communications while working as a lead technician for a small IT company in Tequesta, FL called Allstate Sales & Leasing. In 2003, he was offered the opportunity to acquire the IT company. He purchased the assets of Allstate Sales & Leasing, combined them with Netrodyne's, and founded Allstate Computers.

Today, Allstate Computers is a managed IT services provider located in Jupiter, FL. Allstate specializes in providing security-first IT solutions, network management, and cloud services. The businesses they serve range from 3 to over 300 employees. Brian and his team have developed a proven IT and cyber security compliance, and risk management program designed to eliminate the burden of managing and securing IT systems that business owners are forced to deal with. Allstate's mission is to partner with its clients to transform their IT systems from a necessary evil into a tool for success.

Allstate Computers

(561) 743-1521 / (855) IT-GURUS

www.allstatecomputers.com

Three Security Measures Your Business Needs Now

By Christopher Bartosz

For years, cyber security consisted of having antivirus on your computer and maybe an IT person on-call to fix computer problems. Today, the threats have changed, and the attack vectors have changed. A good security practice requires multiple layers that are monitored and acted upon consistently. Just having an IT professional on-call to fix a computer problem isn't enough anymore. You want to have a team on your side, looking for attacks and doing everything possible to prevent someone from walking right into your computer systems. Over the years, I have seen companies using free antivirus programs, no firewalls, and no one proactively monitoring their computer systems. I have walked into businesses that have no budget for IT and think of IT as just another expense to be cut. In reality, computers are an essential part of your business and they need to be cared for. I have talked with multiple business owners who tell me they are not a target and they have nothing anyone would want. When we dive deeper into their business, there is always something hackers would want — bank account information or customer data, for example.

The first step in having a good cyber security practice is knowing where you are today. To get the most comprehensive look into your security, you need to have an outside third party perform a cyber security assessment. A comprehensive look includes more than answering just a few questions like, do you have antivirus, or have you installed a firewall? This assessment should include performing phishing testing on all employees, checking for any personal identifiable information (PII) that is stored on all computers and in the cloud, checking to see if each and every computer and server on the network is properly configured, making sure your cloud environment (Microsoft 365) is set up securely, and testing the capabilities of your firewall. I have talked with some business owners who tell me they went to the cloud so they are "fine." But the cloud is not perfect. If set up incorrectly, your cloud data is open to anyone on the internet. Microsoft is always changing their systems by adding new security options. This cyber assessment will expose any holes that are out there.

With all of the changes happening in cyber space, one measure to take right away is to review your policies and procedures. Technology is known to change all the time; are you updating your procedures at least yearly to reflect the changing environment? Are you training your employees on your policies and procedures? Are you providing cyber security training to your employees? Typically, the businesses I have seen that do train their employees do it once a year and in a big chunk. While this may seem like a great way to save time, it is creating a gap in your security. To make the training more effective, it is best to train in smaller chunks. It is important to have your employees review your company's policies and procedures once a year, but also add in weekly micro training. This takes about two to five minutes a week. Employees watch a short video and take a micro quiz on the topic. This is an excellent way to increase your cyber hygiene within your company. You can turn this into a friendly competition within your company to see which employee has the highest score!

Why is training so important? Think about the other aspects of your business. Do you have policies or procedures around bringing in new clients or providing services to your existing client base? What about new employees? You don't hire someone, sit them down and say, "Get to work!" You have a procedure to train them so they service your clients the way you want them to.

Another important measure is to make sure you are adequately protected with insurance. It is important to have business insurance, but also a separate cyber security insurance policy. I have talked with multiple business owners who tell me they don't need it. I have also spoken to insurance brokers who say their clients don't need a cyber policy. Why is this so important? Typical business policies do not cover the cost of a cyber event, but they cover your business in other ways. From your cyber security assessment, you should get a risk score. This risk score should also have a dollar amount tied to it. This is your overall risk in the event your business gets hacked and data is taken from you. Specific cyber security policies will cover the cost of third-party forensics, costs associated with notifying your clients, or cover the costs of providing credit monitoring to your clients.

A couple of years ago, getting attacked meant removing the virus from your computer and moving on. Today, hackers dig deep into your data, encrypt it, and in some cases, steal it from you and sell it. What is your clients' data worth to you?

Think of your security as an onion. Why? Because onions have layers and your security should be layered. We already discussed the assessment, employee training, and insurance. What about the actual security of your computer? Are you thinking antivirus? Antivirus programs are typically reactive software, only kicking into action once they detect something. Today, we use advanced endpoint protection. That sounds fancy, but what is it? Advanced endpoint protection is proactive because it actively hunts for attacks and threats. It looks at the behaviors of programs to see if they are doing something they shouldn't be doing. For example, if you open Word, a command prompt or script should not try to run at the same time. An antivirus program won't detect that action, but the advanced endpoint protection would notice something unusual like that and stop it. Is that all you need then? Well, no, it goes deeper than that. Think of the onion. There is no one magical product that will stop everything. We layer on top additional software that hunts for other threats that may be sitting idle on your computer. It usually takes hackers months of being on your computer before they launch their attacks; we need something to hunt them out before they can launch any kind of attack. There are literally hundreds of products on the market that claim to protect your computers. Technology changes, and your security software needs to change with it to provide the best possible protection. This new security software also needs to be monitored and adjusted regularly. Gone are the days of installing your favorite antivirus program and forgetting about it until it is time to renew.

Today, it is not a matter of "if" but "when" you get attacked. Having an incident response plan will help you when something happens. This plan should include the steps needed to recover your technology systems, but also all the contacts that need to be informed. Your first calls will be to your cyber security insurance provider and your managed services provider. Why do you need to contact your insurance company when you just want to be back up and running as quickly as possible? Your insurance company will want to collect evidence, and, quite possibly, they will retain the help of an outside provider to do a complete forensic analysis of the event. They will be looking for attack vectors and try to determine if any data was taken out of the company. If data was taken from your company, you will need the assistance of your insurance company to minimize any damages.

Computers are an essential part of any business and they are here to stay. Knowing where you are at today and putting together a plan to get to where you want to be is essential. Employees are seen by hackers as the weakest link in your company, but you can change that. Having a training program and engaging your employees is important. Protect your business by having adequate cyber security insurance, reviewing your policies and procedures, having advanced protections put on your computers, and having a cyber assessment done!

About the Author

Christopher Bartosz is the President and CEO of FVC Technologies based out of Chicago, IL. FVC Technologies focuses on servicing small- to mid-sized businesses as their out-sourced IT department in Chicagoland and across the nation by providing IT management and cyber security solutions. Together with business owners, Christopher works to develop a technology plan that will grow and change with the company. The plans focus on keeping the company secure and implementing innovative technologies to improve efficiency within the organization. He has extensive knowledge of multiple government regulations that he uses to ensure his clients who hold government contracts remain compliant and secure.

Christopher believes that people should never stop learning. He participates in frequent continuing education to stay up-to-date on technology and security solutions. He is also a Microsoft partner and can transform your workplace productivity by introducing you to the new Microsoft ecosystem through the implementation of a customized Share-Point solution for your business. He also provides education and security training to the companies he serves.

When not working with other business owners, Christopher unwinds by spending time with his wife, Kelly, and their dogs. Together they enjoy travelling to unfamiliar places and exploring local cuisine. Christopher also enjoys staying fit by golfing or running and has completed the Chicago Marathon, although his favorite race is the 5K.

Take a risk assessment at cyber.fvctechnologies.com.

www.fvctechnologies.com

The Truth About How Hackers Exploit Your Business

By Chuck Dornon

I woke up to a beautiful morning on a nice crisp day in October in the Willamette Valley here in Oregon. I was getting myself settled into the office and received a call from a previous customer we supported for a brief period in another state, many years prior. They were reaching out about a very bad situation they were in. Through a very brief conversation, it sounded very likely that they were infected by a worm-able ransomware package that got around some of their basic firewall and exchange policies and rules. This previous customer was someone that had declined a more comprehensive security and monitoring package with us and decided to look for other providers that suited their budget. We decided we needed to protect ourselves and our business and amicably discontinued supporting and contractually working with them at that time as well.

After that brief discussion, I was told they hired a "junior IT person" to handle their medical clinic's information technology shortly after we broke ties with them. We were essentially asked what they should do about all of it — they were asking us for help. Knowing our past relationship, we declined to help them because we felt that even if we cleaned this up, the company would not change practices or invest more into their security infrastructure and processes. We decided to forward them on to another group we work closely with that could help them mitigate their issue.

We later found out the worm got in like most malware does, through email. As silly as email is today — it feels like the next version of faxing — it is still around, and it is still, sadly, the largest attack vector for ransom gangs and hackers. On top of that, we learned because this company was using an on-premises mail server that was upgraded and misconfigured by the junior IT employee, it was possibly the most likely reason for this attack. And the problem factors were much deeper from what we initially heard. They had a misconfigured SPF 7 record, and someone chose not to set up DKIM, which is just a simple email authentication method. The junior IT employee migrated domains for this business but never set up the rest of the necessary bits to have proper authentication and more control externally and internally.

At the end of the day, they found out that an internal HR member had her email account spoofed. The hackers were sending spoofed internal emails throughout the company. Emails skipped DKIM because it was nonexistent and skipped SPF because it was not setup properly.

Obviously, internal employees were trusting this account, the emails, and attachments. The hackers were sending these late in the evening, most likely knowing some staff would still be charting patient files at these times. From our understanding, these attachments were HR related and the naming cadence was like other reports HR sends out to specific employees. At this point, I think the company we referred the clinic to knew their entire system needed to be wiped out and set up from scratch: servers, PCs, and possibly mobile devices. But strangely, the clinic declined and wanted them to try preserving their systems.

Why would they decline? People with my experience know why: because they did not have a proper business continuity device, plan, or solid backups to restore from. The organization also realized they would lose a lot of money with head count and employees not working, and at the same time, a slow mitigation potentially loses a company more in that realm. The IT security company we referred them to tried their best to clean up and mitigate. For many months, it sounded like what they did worked, and the client was looking into better backups and moving their dated on-premises mail system to the cloud. I was happy to hear it, because I really enjoy a positive story where the good guys win and the hackers lose. I didn't care who did the work for this clinic, just that their security was fixed and secured so future issues could be minimized.

The company had new measures in place, better business processes that are more security oriented, backup continuity solutions in place, and training for users. A lot changed for the positive. But then month seven comes around, and the EDR in place and other signature-based security warnings start to alert the company that the infection, Emotet, is back. What they found was that Emotet was lying dormant on a laptop that was never cleaned up properly. It was trying to connect to an entirely new set of command-and-control servers. But at this time, the gateway security would not allow it to perform the actions it needed to infect further.

Emotet creates a back door into systems via phishing email campaigns — email spoofing campaigns. These campaigns send out various file types to the receivers, usually in the form of Microsoft Word (.doc) documents. The people behind Emotet rent infected machines out to hackers or "script kiddies" as a portal for more malware attacks. Emotet at the time could lay dormant on a machine and when the portal for attack wants to be opened, the attacker gets direct access to the machine and starts launching remote access commands, or secure shell commands, to the machine to essentially wake up services, and open ports so other trojans and services can drop in. Emotet evolved from a trojan to a trojan dropper, giving attackers a gateway to additional attack types throughout a network.

But what was happening at this clinic was so strange, I could not even understand what they were telling me. It was 2016 and we had very little data on how it worked at this time. What they were witnessing was that email threads and even some email content within good emails between internal and external recipients were being hijacked with malicious links.

Let's say one user sends an email to the front desk about a patient resource online that is a URL link. The front desk opens the email or secure messaging, imports the link into the patient's messaging for their patient's portal, then off the message goes to the patient. What just happened was that Emotet just vectored to a new external account. A patient potentially has a malicious link in their chart that they will open on a personal or work device of their own. Now Emotet can spread from one organization to many others. Luckily, for this clinic, it never got outside of their internal systems before it was once again mitigated. The junior IT employee did some good by figuring out the external IP address and the range the command-and-control server was connecting to at the time. He created a firewall rule to block traffic to that range, essentially creating a communication block between the infected company and the external Emotet servers controlling the attack. You can see how easily this malware worm could have spread outside the clinic. He might have opened up the company to the attack, but he helped greatly by blocking access to those command-and-control servers.

At that time, the business finally decided it would be best to do a controlled wipe of their systems so they could finally be clear of the monster known as Emotet. Many EMR servers, file servers, fax servers, PCs, laptops, and specific mobile devices all were eventually wiped to stock. That is a big financial decision when you do not have backups you can trust. But this business was incredibly lucky to the extent that they are still operating today.

Five years later, this clinic is running strong again. We do not manage or support them; the company that did the clean up now supports their systems. The mail systems are now in the cloud, the EMR is in the cloud, and for any other on-premises critical devices, the clinic is using some great business continuity and backup devices that are on-premise and in the cloud. They have extensively retooled the clinic for very regulated processes with security always top-of-mind.

Now this story I have laid out is not the usual. 60% of small businesses go out of business within six months of an attack, according to many sources.[6] This business should have gone out of business, but they had an

---

[6] https://www.vox.com/sponsored/11196054/why-every-small-business-should-care-about-cyber-attacks-in-5-charts

amazing group of talented IT professionals that saved them. IT groups like them deal with similar situations very regularly, and they know exactly what to do and suggest. The problem is the IT firm does not always make the end choices a business takes. We can protest, and explain the reasons why we suggest certain measures, but at the end of the day, it is our job as IT consultants and cyber security experts to lay out the pros and cons and it's the business' choice to implement or not.

If you are the IT consultant and you are not presenting your solutions in a way that make business sense to the owners, administrator, or c-suites, then you get the situation I laid out about the clinic. Even though the IT consultant was correct, the choice made by the business was what they felt they needed to do to keep operating while clean-up was performed. As of this date, the company supporting this clinic has active dark web monitoring for all employees and domains they own. They have file and disk encryption running across all devices. They also now have an excellent file retention, logging, auditing process, and software package that will alert them to many possible threats, including Emotet signatures.

Now the story above to me is a very good scenario to show how something negative can turn into a positive for a business, and if the business is lucky, they have not exposed patient data or had patient data stolen. But this is not the norm.

In the first half of 2021, we have had more than all the malware infections in the entirety of 2020. Up 30% for the prior calendar year according to the U.S. Treasury Financial Crimes and Enforcement Network with recent attacks targeting various sectors, including manufacturing, legal, insurance, health care, energy, education and the food supply chain in the United States and across the globe. Treasury Secretary Janet L. Yellen recently noted in a Sep 21, 2021 press release by the U.S. Department of the Treasury that "ransomware and cyber-attacks are victimizing businesses large and small across America and are a direct threat to our economy."[7]

I have underlined the sentence above because the clinic's event I wrote about was directly affected by human error on many levels. But at the end of the day, those human errors were made on the pretense of someone trying to maliciously take advantage and criminally profit off others' loss and potential downfall. Even though human error happened and the junior IT employee made a large mistake, he should have never been in that position to start with. It was oversight of management based on budget and many other operational facts. Sadly, that direction exposed their business, employees, and patients to huge risks. Additionally, the employees for this business needed better phishing and malware identification training and just better overall better company IT hygiene.

---

[7] https://home.treasury.gov/news/press-releases/jy0364

I stated above that 60% of businesses, after being hit with a cyber attack, only survive for six months after. But very little is talked about regarding what happens to the businesses that try to stay in business. In some cases, this can be worse. You have people limping infected systems along, trying to maintain businesses with systems crippled, and employees starting to lose trust in the business they work for. If clients or patients are notified without the proper steps, then the lawsuits start to pile up, you lose credibility in your industry, you lose your customers' trust and possibly your investors. Your systems could be acting or working within a botnet as well. You could be taking other companies down the same road your company is going. The list of negatives goes on and on with a malware example like Emotet.

The road to solving an issue like this is being proactive with a trusted IT security firm or consultant. A managed security service provider like Alexonet is the type of company that can look at your business as a whole, work with management, owners, and stakeholders, to come up with true business continuity plans, procedures, training, and services that work with your business model, operation goals, compliance bodies, and budget.

Luckily, in January 2021, the Emotet botnet and connected infrastructure was taken down in an internationally coordinated effort by Europol and Eurojust. The operation was followed up with arrests made in Ukraine and Great Britain.

The lesson I have learned with my experience doing IT security for 22 years is this: when one incredibly crafty threat goes away another that is more thought out, more evasive, and more devasting to those infected rears its ugly head. With the proliferation of crypto currency, we may never see an end to ransomware, botnets, malicious crypto mining, droppers, and so many more. But if we keep our IT hygiene high, our backup and disaster solutions and processes within best practices, our employees continuously trained, we start to take the power back from these criminals. The clinic's situation could have been much worse — if they had exposed all patient data, they most likely would have been out of business. Paying for credit protection, and dark web monitoring for a patient list of over 2500 could mean devastating outcomes for even the most profitable companies.

Good luck; it's dangerous out there, but you have guides out there that want to help you achieve success!

About the Author

Born in Burbank, California, Chuck Dornon has made Oregon his home for over 40 years. Chuck is an avid classic car and Mustang enthusiast. When Chuck is not tinkering away on one of his classic Mustangs or working on his award winning '69 Mustang Grande, he spends his time modifying and shooting firearms. He enjoys coming up with new creative creations on his swarm of 3D printers as well. Chuck additionally takes a lot of his free time helping cancer patients any way he can throughout the Willamette Valley and greater Oregon. Chuck comes from a family of successful entrepreneurs, like his grandfather, who owned a conglomeration of TV stations in Southern Oregon. Before Chuck started Alexonet, he enjoyed a satisfying and educational career working for Nortel Networks as a senior network engineer. Chuck has over 22 years' experience in IT and information security. Alexonet has been in business for over 25 years and is regarded as the top MSP & MSSP in the area. He prides himself on a hard work ethic, honesty, integrity, and open communication.

Contact: Chuck Dornon

Alexonet

133 NE Dunn Place, McMinnville, Oregon 97128

Phone: 503-883-9046

https://alexonet.com

Security 101: What Can You Do to Protect Your Business from the Unknown?

By Mike Bloomfield

Close your eyes and begin to relax. Now imagine you are lying in bed, sleeping peacefully and you begin to open your eyes to find an intruder standing over you. How would this make you feel? How could this happen to you? Your first thought would be that they broke in, or did they? You made the decision to leave your front door wide open; why would you expect differently?

We all know the above is absolute fiction because no one reading this would remove their front door while they are sleeping. Now let me ask the same question about your business security stance. Have you implemented a Zero Trust security model within your business environment? "No," you answer. So if you wouldn't remove the front door when you go to bed, why would you remove the front door protecting your business infrastructure?

Let's start with explaining the Zero Trust security model as defined by the National Security Agency:

> *Zero Trust is a security model, a set of system design principles, and a coordinated cybersecurity and system management strategy based on an acknowledgement that threats exist both inside and outside traditional network boundaries. The Zero Trust security model eliminates implicit trust in any one element, node, or service and instead requires continuous verification of the operational picture via real-time information fed from multiple sources to determine access and other system responses.*

Further continuing the definition, the NSA goes on to say that the Zero Trust security model assumes that a breach is inevitable or has likely already occurred, so it constantly limits access to only what is needed.

In previous security models, IT professionals relied on antivirus software to detect when a virus was running. The virus needed to run and begin processing its code to be caught and eliminated. It's no different than if you had opened your eyes and simply asked the intruder to leave your home, but we all know it's much better to simply not ever have that intruder gain access. With Zero Trust, the virus would not even be able to launch and run, as it would not be on the whitelist for applications that can be run within the environment. Should it accidently be whitelisted and allowed to run, this is where endpoint security solutions come in today, to stop the process that was allowed to run. However, the odds that it would even be allowed to run is greatly reduced.

The Zero Trust security model should be the foundation for any modern cyber security strategy that stands a chance against the cyber terrorists in 2021 and beyond. As with any cyber security strategy, it starts with a risk assessment. A risk assessment can be completed by a managed service provider and will break down the risk in your organization, both digitally and physically. This risk assessment is the same as how your medical doctor would perform an examination and lab tests prior to prescribing medicine. From the risk assessment, you'll be able to see exactly where your organization falls in various categories and see recommendations on areas to improve to get your risk lowered.

The best way to lower risk is to adopt the Zero Trust security model along with a multi-layered security approach. Just as a prison has multiple safeguards in place to prevent a prisoner from getting out, your security model must have multiple safeguards in place to prevent hackers from getting in. This multi-layered approach must start at the most common entry point of most breaches, your email. More than

92% of breaches begin by a simple email. To begin your email security layer, you must start with a true business-class email solution, preferably Microsoft 365, or Google Workspace. If you are not on either one of those providers for email, you have already begun leaving windows open in your home for intruders to invade.

Once you are on a business-class email provider, you should now move forward to implement multiple layers of email filtering and phishing protection. The first layer should be an email protection provider that filters both incoming and outgoing emails, as well as implements encrypted secure emails. Most people mistakenly believe that email messages are fully encrypted and that is, unfortunately, false. Email by nature is unencrypted, which is why it's necessary to implement secure email solutions when sending out social security numbers, credit card numbers, other personal information, and attachments.

Once you have protected the first layer, you should now implement an advanced phishing detection solution. These are newer solutions that work to remove zero-day phishing attempts from your mailbox. The top providers in these solutions will use machine imaging to evaluate all links and look for attempts to mimic login phishing pages that are made to look like those of Google, Facebook, Microsoft, etc. These solutions also will attempt to open links sent in an email and run them on a VM (virtual machine) to verify that they are not attempting to download a malware payload or do anything that they shouldn't be doing.

Finally, to protect your business-class email, it is necessary that you implement a backup solution that will back up your cloud tenant. Again, many people falsely believe that when using a cloud provider, the provider is handling all backups. When reading the terms and conditions of both Microsoft and Google, you will see that they do not guarantee your data and recommend you back up your data with a third-party solution.

Now that we have your email protected on multiple fronts and have a backup solution, it's time to begin protecting your networks. To do this, you must replace the routers provided to you by your internet provider and install true business-class firewalls that have the necessary features to protect your network. Such business-class solutions should have features such as virus protection, intrusion prevention, data loss prevention, web content filtering, and application control among other security features.

With your security stack coming together, it's now time to focus on the endpoints. No longer is it adequate to simply install an antivirus solution and call it a day. Now you must install a multi-layered stack on your endpoints that includes various protection suites. To start, you will want to select an advanced endpoint security tool that has AI to monitor your computer processes and can stop processes in their tracks when they go rogue. This advanced endpoint solution should be paired with an active breach monitoring agent. On average, it takes organizations 207 days to become aware that a hacker has breached their network and has an active foothold on the environment. With these active breach monitoring agents, you can know almost immediately should a hacker breach your network and begin setting up a foothold.

Next, we want to get a privilege control solution implemented that allows you to set up your environment with zero administrative access. All privilege requests should be made using a privilege control solution, which allows rules to be built for privilege requests that should be allowed. Consider activities such as opening QuickBooks updates and automatically sending alerts to the help desk for things not recognized or when a rule is not present. By doing this, you are further insuring that even if a payload was downloaded and was attempting to run as the user, the user would not have the administrative access to launch the payload and allow it to begin its destruction.

To continue layering your endpoint stack, you will want to implement a DNS protection suite. DNS is the mechanism that allows you to type an address in your address bar and get to a website. For example, typing in "google.com" will take you to the proper IP address of the google server, thanks to DNS resolution. With a DNS protection suite, you can protect your environment from known malicious domain names and zero-day malware domains among real-time malware by utilizing SSL inspection that comes standard in most of these DNS solutions.

To complete the layering of your endpoint stack, it's time to find a ransomware detection solution. These ransomware detection solutions will monitor your endpoints for an active ransomware attack and kill the process in its tracks. These solutions do this by placing honeypot files around your drives and monitoring these files for any process that attempts to change the file. This becomes the final active protection agent during a ransomware attack before having to go to backups.

With email, the network, and the endpoints covered, it's time to protect any servers that you have with a business continuity solution. With a proper business continuity solution, you should be taking backups on a regular basis, as often as every five minutes during business hours, with backups being stored both locally and in the cloud. This ensures that no matter what type of disaster, you always have access to your dataset. Business continuity is the prevention of downtime, so it's important that your continuity solution allows you to quickly get your servers back up and running virtually in the event of a disaster. With a business continuity solution, you should be able to have extremely low recovery point objectives (RPO) and recovery time objectives (RTO).

The last piece of a well-rounded stack is to train your employees which will ultimately be the weakest link in your security chain. This starts with training, making sure that employees are receiving both annual security training and weekly micro-training to keep them up-to-date on the latest threats they should be aware of. You should be actively phishing your employees and when they fall for the phish, presenting a landing page showing how they could have spotted this attempt in the future and what to look for. It's also extremely important to provide them with a true business-class password management tool so they can properly store their passwords, and with such tools, use different passwords for every site so that they never need to repeat passwords.

Finally, it is necessary to implement multi-factor authentication in all cloud solutions and even local PCs. This ensures that even if their passwords were compromised, they couldn't be used against them for a breach. With 2FA/MFA, even if a password is known and there's an attempt to log in, without the second authentication device like a mobile phone, the hacker will be unable to gain access to the account.

With all the above, you will be well on your way to implementing a Zero Trust security model framework in your organization to protect your assets. However, just knowing the pieces isn't always going to mean you can implement them yourself. Just think of a house, you may know all the pieces needed to build the house, but you may not be able to build the house on your own. So most importantly, the best thing that you can do to protect your organization from the unknown is find a managed service provider who is the expert in securing businesses and lowering their risks. When you hire a managed service provider with a focus on security, they would be the one to implement the required stack. Best of all, you can focus on doing what you do best while they help to secure your business from the unknown.

About the Author

Mike Bloomfield is the President of Tekie Geek, a Managed Service Provider (MSP) head-quartered in Staten Island, NY. Mike is an IT expert throughout the IT community and is regularly published in numerous IT publications including Tech Decisions, ChannelPro Magazine, Channel Executive, and others. In 2020, Mike was also recognized as an Amazon bestselling author for his book, *Hack Proof Your Business - Volume 2*, and again in 2021 for his book, *Stay Calm: How a Crisis Can Strengthen your Business.*

Tekie Geek is an award-winning MSP, with its core services being Managed IT Services, Business Continuity, Cloud Computing, and Unified Communication. With these core services, Tekie Geek is able to cure your IT ailments, properly protect your business from the rising IT threats, and detect issues before they even arise, giving you peace of mind and helping you to sleep better at night. They can do this while maintaining their core company values of Clients, Culture, and Community.

Mike has had a passion for technology since an early age and has continued to push forward to ensure that he is always at the forefront of all technological advances. Before being President Geek of Tekie Geek, Mike has held such positions as IT/Research and Development Director and Manager of Product Engineering in the corporate world.

When Mike isn't focusing on his business, he's spending time with his beautiful wife, Nicole, and daughters, Audriana and Alexis. Mike gives the credit to his family for giving him the drive to keep going strong every day. He's a true geek at heart and it becomes obvious when you start to talk Marvel or Star Wars movies with him. It also becomes obvious when you see his vast collection of collectible figures and statues throughout the Tekie Geek office.

Business Awards

Somerset County Business Partnership Top 40 Under 40

Staten Island Chamber of Commerce Lou Miller Award

SIEDC 20 Under 40 Award

SIEDC Top 31 Businesses in Staten Island

SIEDC Top 31 Fastest Growing Businesses in Staten Island

Star Network King of Staten Island

Star Network Power Duo of Staten Island

Star Network Stars Under 40

Channel Futures MSP 501

Channel Futures NextGen 101

Organizations

Board of Directors, Staten Island Chamber of Commerce

Vice President, Verrazano Kiwanis – Kiwanis Club Of Staten Island

Board of Directors, Meals on Wheels of Staten Island

Board of Directors, Treasurer, Staten Island Business Outreach Center

Board of Directors, Staten Island Board of Realtors

Board of Directors, Co-Chair, South Shore BID

President, The Executive Club of Staten Island

Advisory Board, MailProtector

Advisory Board, CryptoStopper

Contact Details

To schedule a consultation for your Business IT needs, please get in touch with us:

Website: https://www.tekiegeek.com

Client Testimonial Videos: https://love.tekiegeek.com

Email: sales@tekiegeek.com

Facebook: https://facebook.com/tekiegeek

LinkedIn: https://www.linkedin.com/in/mikebloomfield/

Phone: (347) 830-7322

Will My Business be the Next Target for Hackers?

By Shulem Moskovits

Am I really a target for cyber criminals and what is the likelihood my small business will be hacked? David, the CEO of a fast-growing commercial lighting company, had these thoughts from time to time. Being the responsible business owner that he was, he took the initiative and hired an IT consultant to install a good antivirus and backup solution. Now all was good — or so he wanted to believe.

Every time the news broke about the newest hack that just whacked some Fortune 500 company with ransomware or a massive data leak, David knew that it had nothing to do with him. *The bad guys are not looking for my small business, they want the big fish.* Double checking his antivirus software and backup solutions and checking in with a quick phone call to his IT professional, David was assured that all was good – or so he wanted to believe.

On the morning of Dec 31, 2020, right before the new year when everyone was busy prepping for time off with friends and family, the CEO, David, gets a frantic phone call from his assistant, Laura. She can barely speak. Finally, she gets the words out of her mouth, "ALL OUR COMPUTERS AND FILES ARE ENCRYPTED WITH RANSOMWARE!!"

The story above of our CEO, David, is a story that replays itself every single day at different companies in the US and around the world. According to a CNBC survey of small business owners, the key takeaway points are the following:

1. That a majority of America's small business owners are not worried about being the victim of a cyber attack.

2. What's more, small businesses are confident that if they suffered a hack, they would be able to respond to it.

3. And yet, many say they have no formal cyber security response plan in place; some business owners admit they don't even know if their business has a cyber threat plan.[8]

Living in this false sense of security is the primary reason so many businesses are being whacked by cyber criminals. The head-in-the-sand mentality is killing businesses every single day; according to a

---

[8] https://www.cnbc.com/2021/08/10/main-street-overconfidence-small-businesses-dont-worry-about-hacking.html

Cybercrime Magazine article, "60 Percent of Small Companies Close Within 6 Months of Being Hacked."[9]

Most small business owners believe that cyber attacks happen only to multinational companies and that hackers won't come for them, when, in fact, the majority of hacking incidents happen to small- and medium-sized organizations. This past September, the United States Federal Bureau of Investigation (FBI) reported that cyber criminals were focusing their attention on small- to medium-sized businesses, which could come as pretty grim news for smaller businesses that generally don't have the resources, time, or expertise to sufficiently secure their systems.

As someone who has been in the IT and cyber security industry and has been the CEO of SM Tech Solutions for over 10 years, I have seen numerous organizations struggle with protecting their networks and systems from cyber criminals. Every time a company gets hacked and our company is called in to help restore their business operations, the first question that I am asked is, "I thought that we were protected? We paid a yearly fee for our antivirus."

My answer is, "Sorry, having an antivirus is only 10% of the equation."

Below are some security strategies you should adopt in your business to fortify your cyber defense.

---

[9] https://cybersecurityventures.com/60-percent-of-small-companies-close-within-6-months-of-being-hacked/

1. Defense-in-depth: The first security strategy that organizations should be adopting today is called DEFENSE IN DEPTH. The defense-in-depth strategy starts with the notion that every system at some point will fail.

For example, car brakes, airplane landing gear, and even the hinges that hold your front door upright will all eventually fail. The same applies to electronic and digital systems that are designed to keep cybercriminals out, such as, but not limited to, firewalls, antimalware scanning software, and intrusion detection devices. These will all fail at some point.

How can you use this strategy today?

Think about the customer data that you have been entrusted to guard. If a cyber criminal tried to realize unauthorized access to this data, what defense measures are in place to prevent them from getting in? A firewall? If that firewall failed, what is the next implemented action to prevent them from going on? Document each of those layers and add or remove defense layers as necessary. It's entirely up to you each about percentages and therefore the layers of defense to use. What we recommend is that we make that analysis based on a full cyber risk assessment. Clearly understanding the criticality or sensitivity of your systems and data points us toward the final rule: that the more critical or sensitive the system or data is, the more protective layers we must always use.

2. Least privileges

The next security strategy that you can start adopting today is called the LEAST PRIVILEGES strategy. Whereas the defense-in-depth strategy started with the notion that every system will eventually fail, this one starts with the notion that every system can and will be compromised in some way. Using the least privileges strategy, the overall potential damage caused by a cyber criminal attack can be greatly limited.

How can you use this strategy today?

If most accounts in your organization are configured to run as administrators with full rights in a system, this suggests that if a hacker compromises an account, they will have full rights to the entire system. The fact is that most users don't need full rights to a system to perform their responsibilities in your business. By using the smallest amount of privileges strategy today within your organization, you reduce the rights of every computer account to user-level and only grant administrative privileges when needed. Companies like ours will work with your organization to urge your users to configure their accounts using the least-privileges strategy. It's a step you probably won't see the advantages of until you experience a cyber attack, but after you do, you are going to be glad this strategy was implemented.

3. Attack surface reduction

The defense-in-depth strategy previously discussed is used to make the job of a cyber criminal as difficult as possible. The least-privileges strategy is used to limit the damage that a cyber attacker could cause if they managed to hack into a system. With this last strategy, attack surface reduction, the goal is to limit the total possible ways that a cyber criminal could compromise a system.

How can you use this strategy today?

Start by working with your IT team, and for each production system, begin enumerating what network ports, services, and user accounts are enabled on those systems. For each network port, service, and user account identified, a business justification should be identified and documented. If no business justification is identified, then that network port, service, or user account should be disabled.

I could write a whole chapter on each and every one of the above strategies, but I'm not here to bore you with technical details. I wrote this chapter in a way so that you and everyone reading this book can understand the basic concepts of what it takes to implement a robust cyber security program in their business.

If you are asking yourself, "How and where do I even start? This technical stuff is so complicated," then you should know that help is out there and many great IT/cyber security service providers exist that have extensive knowledge. They can guide you step-by-step on how to secure your business network. The following are four tips on how to choose the right cyber security firm.

1. Their primary focus should be on cyber security.

In the past, IT professionals were mostly focused on the productivity of their clients, making sure that all their systems work as expected at all times and they put little emphasis on cyber security. But today, a good IT service provider's main focus should be on cyber security and the secondary focus should be on productivity.

2. They don't prescribe before diagnosing.

You wouldn't trust a doctor that prescribes medication before they do a thorough physical exam; the same goes for an IT service provider. Stay away from an IT service provider that will propose a cyber security package before they have performed an extensive cyber risk assessment and understand all the aspects of your business.

3. They're NOT the cheapest out there.

We all know the saying, "you get what you pay for." If you are looking to find the cheapest guy on the street to protect your business, then put away the money you saved for when you get hacked. The fact is, there is no way anyone can protect you properly and still be the cheapest.

4. They desire a long-term relationship.

It takes time and effort to implement an effective cyber security plan, and then it has to be maintained on a regular basis. So make sure you choose a cyber security firm that has been in business for at least five years, and is stable and willing to be your partner for a long time to come.

I hope I gave you some useful tips on what it takes to protect your business and data from the bad guys, but remember, "perfection is the enemy of good." No cyber security plan is perfect, but having no plan at all is financial suicide, so go out there and find a cyber security firm to help and advise you on how to protect your business from cyber criminals.

***

If you have any questions, you are more than welcome to email me at Shulem@smtechsolutions.com or reach out to me via LinkedIn: www.linkedin.com/in/shulem-moskovits.

About the Author

Fascinated by everything tech from a very young age, Shulem Moskovits' love for technology landed him in New Horizon Information technology school at the age of 19, where he got his CompTIA and Microsoft certifications.

Shulem founded SM Tech Solutions, a Managed IT Service company servicing the SMB market in New York and New Jersey in 2011, with the purpose and goal of consulting and helping business owners grow their businesses by utilizing technology to its best abilities, and offering a one-stop shop for all things technology. (Networking, Cyber Security, Cloud hosting, Dev ops, VoIP solutions, etc.)

From a one-man band, SM Tech Solutions grew into a team of highly talented IT professionals offering a wide range of services with a strong focus on cyber security, with clients spanning across the United States and Canada.

Besides being CEO and leading the company, the majority of Shulem's workday is dedicated to Cyber Security, developing proprietary security solutions, and making sure that his clients are secure from crippling cyber attacks.

Shulem currently lives in Lakewood New Jersey with his wife Shifra and 5 beautiful kids which he loves spending quality time with.

Shulem can be reached at shulem@smtechsolutions.com or on Linkedin at www.linkedin.com/in/shulem-moskovits

Cyber Security Deep Dive: Are Your Employees The Weakest Link?

By Brett Gallant

From the time COVID struck, organizations — irrespective of their size — have become exponentially more vulnerable to cyber threats, triggered by the shift to remote-working. Our ever-increasing reliance on remote technology, networks, software, and even social media, can inadvertently invite cyber attacks, resulting in a catastrophic loss of business and personal data. But, what's the biggest threat to your cyber security? You and the people you work with.

You may think we're talking about disgruntled employees — which can certainly be the case — but, more commonly, it's you and your trustworthy coworkers: owners and employees who haven't been trained to identify the ever-changing cyber threats or to take precautions related to cyber security.

I started my IT career with my first official job back in 1996. Even back then, the threats of ransomware and cyber attacks were real, but not as prolific as they are today. Currently, I own and manage Adaptive Office Solutions, which caters to the business community in Eastern Canada.

Our specialty is cyber security, and our clients range from pharmacy chains to credit unions, and everything in between. Because our clientele is so diverse, we tailor our cyber security risk assessments to meet the unique needs of each business in our portfolio.

I live in a small community, along with my wife and five children, in Northern New Brunswick, Canada. Just like any other community, when we speak of cyber security, there's that belief that *"It can never happen to me. Can never happen to my business. The hackers are not coming after me."* But the reality is, hackers are going after everyone, and their skillset is, unfortunately, improving at a breakneck pace.

A few statistics that hit close to home are: Ransomware attacks increased 10.7 times between July, 2020 and June of 2021.[10] Another staggering statistic is that 50% of small and mid-sized businesses have experienced at least one cyber attack in the last

---

[10] https://www.fortinet.com/content/dam/fortinet/assets/threat-reports/report-threat-landscape-2021.pdf

year. And 94% of business leaders say they're concerned about ransomware.[11]

Do you know how these things happen? There's a variety of ways, but the biggest risk to your business is your people. 94% of malware is delivered via email.[12] For 10 employees, that's an average of 90 email-borne malware threats per month.[13] And, one in 323 emails are malicious. Also, 81% of small to medium businesses report that new types of attacks have evaded their traditional security solutions like antivirus.[14] So, we have a new cyber reality, and the reality is... they're targeting victims just like you.

To be sure the cyber security measures you have in place are adequate for your business, regular security assessments must be scheduled to identify internal and external threats. Without them, security gaps can expose the company's data to hackers and weaken system operations, resulting in financial loss and irreparable damage to your business and reputation.

You may wonder why a cyber security assessment is necessary. In short, the assessments help to identify vulnerabilities within your infrastructure, including

---

[11] https://www.fundera.com/resources/small-business-cyber-security-statistics

[12] https://www.fundera.com/resources/small-business-cyber-security-statistics

[13] ibid

[14] https://pcs-hsv.com/times-have-changed#:~:text=81%25%20of%20SMBs%20report%20new%20types%20of%20attacks%20have%20evaded%20traditional%20security%20solutions%2C%20like%20antivirus

(but not limited to): malware, unpatched security, hidden backdoor programs, software bugs, IoT devices, and... employee error.

Identifying Cyber Security Vulnerabilities

There are countless IT security vulnerabilities for every business. When you consider all of the computers, tablets, smart phones, printers, etc., that are connected to multiple networks (on and offsite), each device is exposed to cyber security threats in their own unique way. It would be impossible (and mind-numbing for you) to list them all.

Knowing there are a lot of moving parts when it comes to identifying all of the potential threats to your cyber security, we'll stick to the most critical things to assess:

- **Malware** - The goal of malicious malware is to access sensitive data. Basic antivirus can protect against some malware, but a multitiered security solution should include: antivirus, deep packet inspection, filtering firewalls, intrusion detection systems, email virus scanners, and employee awareness training. They must run in tandem in order to provide optimal protection.

- **Unpatched Security Vulnerabilities** - Unpatched vulnerabilities allow attackers to run malicious code by leveraging an unpatched security bug they discover in the software protection you use. The task of patching software vulnerabilities is a never-ending process, but organizations must have a well-defined strategy in place to minimize threats to sensitive company data. When you are notified that a new version of your antivirus or malware protection software is available, be sure to update your devices immediately.

- **Hidden Backdoor Programs** - Backdoor installations take advantage of vulnerable components in a web application. Once installed, detection is difficult, as the trojans — typically masquerading as an email attachment or file — tend to adapt to their environment making them virtually invisible. Cyber criminals use this method to steal personal and financial data, install additional malware, and hijack devices.

- **Admin Account Privileges** - The less information employees can access, the less damage they can do — intentionally or otherwise. It's imperative to put security measures in place — unique to each team member — that block access to information that is not necessary for them to do their job. This is critical for managing computer security vulnerabilities. And, don't forget to remove all privileges when an employee has left the company.

- **Automated Running of Scripts Without Malware/Virus Checks** - Some attackers use certain web browsers that run scripts automatically, without requiring a malware or virus scan. As a result, cyber criminals get the browser to run malware without the knowledge of the user. Because these fileless attacks exist only in the computer's memory, traditional static file detection is rendered useless. Scripts also complicate post-event analysis because traces of the attack may be overwritten or removed through a reboot.

- **Unknown Bugs in Software or Programming Interfaces** - A coding defect is known as a software bug that can be used by hackers to gain unauthorized access to a computer system through any number of the software applications you use. Software bugs can introduce security vulnerabilities to every device your company's employees use. The earlier vulnerabilities are exposed, the sooner security teams can analyze the risk and take the necessary steps to patch them.

- **Phishing Attacks** - Phishing is a type of social engineering attack often used to steal user data, including login credentials and credit card numbers. It occurs when an attacker, masquerading as a trusted entity, lures a victim into opening an email or text message. The recipient is then tricked into clicking a malicious link. This can lead to the installation of malware, holding your system hostage — as part of a ransomware attack or the stealing of sensitive information.

- **Your IoT Devices** - IoT (Internet of Things) devices are insecure by design, because they lack the processing power for basic protection, like encryption. It's likely that IoT will become the number one source for ransomware attacks in the very near future. Botnets, advanced persistent threats, distributed denial of service (DDoS) attacks, identity theft, data theft, man-in-the-middle attacks, and social engineering attacks are all possible when using IoT devices.

- **Human Error -** Employees may click on a malicious link in an email, download a corrupted file, visit an unsecure website, or share credentials with the wrong people, allowing hackers easy access to your company's sensitive data. Ongoing cyber security training helps employees identify the ever-emerging cyber security threats so they won't become victims of cyber crimes. By keeping their devices protected, they will also be protecting your business' sensitive data.

Identifying security vulnerabilities allows you to fix potential weaknesses in your organization's cyber security network, thereby protecting you from cyber attacks. The main objective is to continuously fix the security gaps before attackers use them to create a cyber security breach.

Cyber security vulnerabilities and threats are always changing. Every day, new vulnerabilities and exploits are discovered. Doing vulnerability testing and providing immediate solutions are crucial for putting an end to new cyber security threats each time they arise.

Now that you've read the short list of potential threats to your cyber security, let's take a closer look at some mistakes your business may be making, and how and why you should consider making some changes.

Cyber Attack Prevention

Training Employees

Employees put their company's data or systems at risk when they do not have the required training to understand the latest cyber threats that can harm the business they work for. In fact, 46% of cybersecurity incidents last year were due to employee error.[15] What should they avoid?

Here's a short list:

- Avoid clicking on suspicious links

- Don't open or download email attachments from an unknown sender

---

[15] https://www.kaspersky.com/blog/the-human-factor-in-it-security/#:~:text=In%20addition%2C%20in%2046%25%20of%20cybersecurity%20incidents%20in%20the%20last%20year%2C%20careless/%20uniformed%20staff%20have%20contributed%20to%20the%20attack.

- Never click on pop-ups

- Use a strong password system, with two-factor authentication

- Do not visit unsecure websites (check for the lock icon in the search bar)

Login Credentials and Passwords

Every employee needs their own unique login credentials. Several users connecting with the same password can put your business at risk. Having unique logins for staff member visits will help you reduce the number of cyber risks.

- Employees should never share their login information

- Login information should be stored in a secure digital platform for each user

- Be sure to delete login credentials when an employee is no longer with the company

Creating a strong computer password or phrase is perhaps the easiest way to enhance the security of your system. Set up a complex password or phrase from 8 to 64 alphanumeric characters, and use special characters such as "#@*&." Remember, passwords should never be written down and stored near your device. When possible, adopt a two-factor authentication strategy.

At Adaptive Office Solutions, we suggest using Keeper Security. Keeper manages your passwords to prevent data breaches, improve employee productivity, cut help desk costs, and meet compliance standards.

- All employees should have their own unique login credentials for every service and app they use. This simplifies access control and enables IT admins to apply granular security policies on the user level.

- Don't skimp on security measures for shared passwords. Enable multi-factor authentication (2FA) on all accounts that support it. Cyber criminals won't be able to access the account without the second factor.

- Reset shared passwords whenever someone leaves the company. Keeper enables admins to disable accounts and reset shared passwords within minutes.

IT Security Policy

Your IT security policy should be the go-to resource that mitigates threats. A comprehensive policy should cover the education of employees, protocols for a threat or breach, and how employees should protect valuable data, whether on-site or remotely. Your IT security policy should also address issues regarding BYOD (bring your own device) rules, establish cyber security regulations, and include step-by step-instructions when facing a threat.

A cyber security policy should include:

- A list of confidential data

- Device security measures for company and personal use

- Email security

- Data transfer measures

- Disciplinary action, should the rules be ignored

Bring Your Own Device and Remote Working

Many people use their own devices (BYOD) into the workplace. But, downloading and accessing data and sensitive information can compromise your company's data if their device lacks the same level of security that your business has established. Additionally, employees who work from home and log into your network remotely, can breach your organization's cyber security.

Steps employees should take to safeguard company data:

- Connect to secure Wi-Fi (via a VPN) whenever accessing company data

- Install a firewall, antivirus, malware protection, and advanced endpoint protection

- Make sure software and operating systems are automatically updated

- Never link a business account to your personal account

- Enable 2FA/MFA on devices and systems when available

Yes... even cellphones need to be safeguarded.

Cloud Applications

The cloud offers considerable advantages over traditional on-site or physical data storage: from significantly increased data storage capacity and cost-effectiveness, to easy accessibility and collaboration. But what most people don't know is that hackers can access all of that information, too. So, unless you want to become a victim of a ransomware attack, it is essential to have a cyber security IT partner who will encrypt and secure your data from internal and external threats.

What can you do to ensure data security in the cloud? In addition to the tips already listed:

- Read the user agreement thoroughly before you sign up

- Don't upload personal information (such as your birthday, your mother's maiden name, your children's school or activity schedules, etc.)

- Don't store sensitive information (credit card numbers, passwords, passport info, etc.)

Disaster Recovery Plan

The impact of data loss or corruption from hardware failure, human error, natural disasters, cyber crime, and infected software could have a significant impact on your business. Should a breach take place and data is wiped, corrupted, or held for ransom, a disaster recovery plan ensures that you can minimize losses. A disaster recovery plan — in addition to an IT security policy — helps your business respond quickly and recover as soon as possible; minimizing damage and costly downtime.

At minimum, your disaster recovery plan should include the following steps:

- Know your threats
- Identify your assets
- Use data replication redundancy — store on hard drives, save in the cloud, export to encrypted flash drives, utilize hybrid cloud storage
- Test backups and restoration of services on a regular basis

Partner With an IT Cyber Security Specialist

The amount of digital data has increased exponentially over the last few years. At the same time, hackers have become immeasurably more skilled. So, neglecting to partner with a cyber security specialist could literally cost you your business, affecting the lives of everyone involved.

There is a clear need to perform threat assessments and implement cyber security measures to reduce your organization's risk of cyber attacks. Protection against cyber threats is an investment, but it's not nearly as expensive as the cost of losing all of your data. It's no longer enough to rely on traditional technology protection or security controls for information security.

Data that could historically be addressed with IT risk *management*, now needs to be protected by well-trained cyber security professionals, revolutionary software applications and rigorous cyber attack prevention.

Using a multi-layered approach, cyber security specialists use their expertise and up-to-date knowledge to help protect against web threats that facilitate cyber crime including: malware, phishing, viruses, denial-of-service attacks, information warfare, and hacking.

In a beautifully written excerpt by Florida Tech Online, they write:

Cyber security specialists are responsible for keeping cyber crime at bay by using their proficiency in analysis, forensics, and reverse engineering to monitor and diagnose malware events and vulnerability issues.

They then make recommendations for solutions, including hardware and software programs that can help mitigate risk. These professionals typically design firewalls, monitor use of data files, and regulate access to safeguard information and protect the network.

Staying up-to-date on current virus reports and protecting networks from these viruses is a major aspect of a cybersecurity specialist's job duties. They often train users, promote security awareness, develop policies and procedures, and provide updates and reports to management and executive staff."[16]

Conclusion

Since the onset of COVID, businesses have become significantly more vulnerable to cyber attacks. The landscape shifted dynamically when employees were required to work remotely. In the past, business owners had much more control over the technology, networks and software they provided. Now, most, if not all, remote workers aren't operating on a single, dedicated business computer that stays in the office and runs exclusively on your secure network. They own multiple devices - most of which are mobile - and they are connecting to new networks, downloading new software, and browsing new internet sites, now more than ever. Then...they connect back into your business network; unwittingly delivering cyber threats that could wreak havoc on your data, your reputation and, ultimately, your business. Don't wait until it's too late to do a cyber security deep dive!

A Checklist:

- Train your staff

---

[16] https://www.floridatechonline.com/blog/information-technology/cybersecurity-specialist-career-guide

- Use email with caution

- Use the internet with caution

- Limit access for each employee

- Assign unique login information

- Utilize a remote password Keeper

- Be mindful of WiFi security: use a VPN at all times, on every device

- Research the basics of computer security

- Backup your data: redundancy is key

- Keep your software and systems fully up-to-date

- Install antivirus software

- Install antispyware and antimalware software; yes, even on cellphones

- Perform daily full-system scans

- Create a periodic, system backup schedule

- Regularly update your computer system

- Use your firewall

About the Author

Brett Gallant has been active in the IT Industry for over 25 years, and has been the owner of Adaptive Office Solutions, in Miramichi, Canada, since the spring of 2010.

Cyber Security is central to Brett's approach. He begins by running a comprehensive, multilayered technology assessment to identify gaps in security, in order to provide sound solutions that solidify the cyber security infrastructure for every client in his portfolio.

His clients include large construction and manufacturing firms to small and medium businesses. Brett takes a customer centric approach, which means the customer is the focal point of all decisions related to delivering products, services, and experiences to create customer satisfaction, loyalty and advocacy. This strategic approach supports his client's goals of running healthy, growing and successful businesses through the use of secure, current and smooth-running technology.

Brett is active in the business and personal community; participating in cyber security groups and volunteering for his church, the Rotary Club of

Chatham, and Camp Sheldrake, a summer camp that empowers youth through meaningful experiences, and develops skills in leadership and community service while increasing spiritual awareness.

He is also one the founding members of BPSA Traditional Scouting in Miramichi, which caters to the outdoor curious, adventurist, pioneer and explorer. Brett has five children, and he and his wife Alison have been happily married since the summer of 2009.

(Author Photo Credit: Denis Duquette – Photographer)

Three Ways to Prevent Getting Hacked

By Andrew Baker

Paul, a business owner of a small firm, received a phone call one Thursday morning from his banking officer, Patty. Patty was calling in response to an email conversation she and Paul had the previous afternoon to authorize his newly-hired financial controller, Larry, to do bank transfers via email request. Oddly, however, Paul had not been emailing Patty and did not hire anyone, let alone a new financial controller named Larry.

Paul's email had fallen victim to a business email compromise (BEC) and a hacker was attempting to exercise a fraudulent funds transfer. One more email would have allowed up to $20,000 to exit Paul's corporate bank account without his knowledge.

At the advice of his bank's manager, Paul quickly acted. He contacted his email provider, changed his password, and uncovered an additional email account for "Larry," which had been created by the hacker. There were also email forwarding rules that moved messages from Paul's inbox into a folder that would **not** notify him of new email received. This is where the impersonated conversation between Patty and the hacker were contained. Upon further inspection of these emails, the hacker had impersonated emojis, grammar, and punctuation that Paul frequently used in his emails. The hacker cloned Paul's email signature, and even forged his written signature when sending the ink-signed and scanned bank note authorizing "Larry" to send money from Paul's bank account at will.

Had this attempt succeeded and the bank officer not called Paul to confirm, "Larry" would have been able to make repeated transfers by sending an email to Patty with only the amount and destination bank account number.

Paul would soon discover this was much more than a close call.

Like so many people, and business owners especially, the contents of Paul's mailbox held every email he had ever sent and received. Passwords to vendors' web portals, scans of tax returns, proof of income, social security numbers, pay stubs with employment information, group benefits IDs, dates of birth, photocopies of his and his wife's driver's licenses were all exposed. The previous year, Paul's family had moved residences and applied for a new mortgage. The entire conversation trail and supporting docu-ments between Paul and his mortgage broker were exposed. Even worse, because Paul's account held admin rights to the email platform, the hacker had also enabled permissions to view the email contents of every other employee of the company and every single document saved in cloud storage for the business.

Unfortunately, only time will show if any of the information is exposed on the dark web, if Paul's credit takes an unexpected loan application, and if the identities of those exposed in his email history will be defrauded in any way. Paul may now be responsible to pay for credit monitoring and identity theft protection to those individuals whose information was stolen. This illustrates how quickly the exposure of a single login credential can become a costly event, and an enormous liability.

Paul is obligated by his state's laws to report the breach of his email account to his business insurance, which fortunately included some cyber security coverage. The insurance investigation uncovered all the information and personal details of his peers/coworkers and any financial records that the hacker would have been able to access. Unfortunately, the exact cause of how his account was targeted and compromised are unknown. His email host only held seven days of access logs, so the origin and date of the breach were long lost. The logs also did not show which files were targeted/downloaded so there's a big unknown on the actual scope of the breach.

In cases like this, it may be wise to assume the worst-case scenario. Assume the hacker downloaded all the files, copied all the emails, and all sensitive documents. Assume the hacker will sell these details on the dark web. Assume the hacker will try to send out impersonating emails to vendors and try to gain further access using the stolen information. Assume the hacker will impersonate Paul from alternative spoofing email accounts and tell vendors that Paul's bank account has changed. The hacker will copy and paste existing email contents, send them to business vendors and redirect money destined to Paul's business to someone else. This is only one of the ways that hackers are profiting from cyber crime.

How did the hacker get into Paul's email? More importantly, how could it have been prevented?

3 Ways to Prevent Being Hacked

Be Invisible Online.

In theory, if we didn't have any computers connected to the internet or have email addresses, we shouldn't be able to fall victim to any cyber crime tactics. Unfortunately, in today's marketplace, it's very difficult — if not impossible — to create and run a successful business without implementing some type of tech-nology with internet exposure. It's even more difficult to advertise without some type of internet branding or social media exposure publishing the company for all to see — both potential buyers and potential hackers.

Let's consider how hackers are currently sourcing targets. In the case of Paul, he doesn't know how his email and password were exposed or why. Paul did admit, however, that he used the same password on several different logons across the internet. This makes it easy for hackers to prey on unsuspecting individuals with online records.

These days, hackers harvest credentials in number of ways — they can log into the dark web and download databases with hundreds of thousands of records for as little as $10. Imagine that; just having your internet email address as part of a database exposes you — and it's worth a fraction of a cent. Robots are deployed to harvest huge database dumps, and phishing emails are sent out to coerce you to divulge your security credentials by using impersonating mock emails. We see these emails, referred to as phishing, being delivered all the time, advising you have a package delivery coming, or that an electronic signed document has been sent to you that you have to log in or create an account to see. Unsuspecting people will enter their common email address and most-used password. That's all it takes. Now their email account can be found and sold on the dark web for over $100, or worse, the hacker will access the email account and all its contents, just like what happened to Paul.

It's possible that Paul clicked on a phishing link in an email sent to him and entered his password. It's also possible that out of a large email database, a robot attempted to brute for his password — this is the act of trying different characters and common passwords and then alerting the hacker of a confirmed sign in. It's also possible that another online website had its user database stolen and the emails and passwords were harvested along with it. Because Paul lacked some minimum security provisions, he was an easy target.

Visit the Dark Web Price Index 2021 to see the Dark Web Prices of Personal Data here: https://www.privacyaffairs.com/dark-web-price-index-2021

We acknowledge it's difficult to be invisible online, but there are ways that we can limit our exposure and make it more difficult for hackers to target or impersonate us.

#1. The first step is to do a web search on yourself. Google, Bing, or Yahoo your first and last name followed by the city you live in. Click on the Images Tab and see which websites expose your face publicly.

ZoomInfo is a website that scrapes information and pictures from LinkedIn. There have been instances where brand new employees at companies start receiving phishing emails within days of being hired and updating their employment status on LinkedIn. This shows that hackers are specifically watching and targeting companies. This enables hackers to prey on someone new by emailing a new hire, impersonating the president or lead controller in accounting and asking to "make a special advance payment."

It's important to contact sites like these which expose employees' names, titles, email addresses, and phone numbers to have your information removed.

#2. Use four email accounts. *Four email accounts? What? But I have everything I need in one!* This means that you have one target for hackers to compromise and it's the gateway to everything.

Anyone using the internet and email for work should maintain four different email accounts (or more), their uses are as follows:

Email #1: Confidential and personal matters. This is the single email address you use for any banking, utility bills, signing into IRS, mortgage documents, health/doctor, group benefits, insurance, prescriptions or highly sensitive information that could be used to compromise your identity or credit. This email address should NEVER be entered on any other website on the internet and should not be distributed or included in any mailing list. The password for this MUST be unique and not be the same or similar to any password of the other two emails. Absolutely use two-factor authentication on this account. If this email is hosted by your internet provider and does not have two-factor authentication, make the effort to change it to Gmail or Outlook. Google and Microsoft have made great strides in adding provisions to notify you of irregular sign-ins and have several options for two factor authentication to ensure your accounts stay safe.

Email #2: Anything with a credit card or payment details. This is the email to use for things like PayPal, AppleID, Amazon, eBay, and your online social media accounts — all the well-acclaimed merchant sites where payment is attached. Although we'd like to think it's unlikely for these accounts to get breached, their size does make them a target. If your credentials get leaked from one of these big providers, at least it's narrowed down only to a couple of merchants. Also, ensure you use different passwords at each of these providers — a password that is again different from this email address' password.

Email #3: This is the SPAM account. Use this email to sign up for newsletters, coupons, or online quizzes that ask you to enter your email to receive the document of interest. Use it to set up any type of online web-based forum, Facebook, or Instagram. There's a chance that websites/online communities can get hacked. The strategy here is that Email #3 has no critical information; if this email falls into the hands of spam lists, it won't affect personal information and limits your exposure.

Pro Tip for Email #3: When signing up for newsletters, rather than using your real first name on the sign-up form, put the name of the website. This way, if you do start receiving unsolicited email, the "Dear *FlashyPajamas.com*" intro will give away which website gave away your email address without permission.

Email #4: Work Email. This is the email address provided to you by your workplace. It also should not be used for anything except for dealings that pertain directly to your business and duties. Use it to only communicate with trusted vendors and coworkers. If there are common accounts needed, like for shipping couriers that others may use, set up an internal shared mailbox that cannot be signed into from the outside such as shipping@companyname.com, then have the Email administrator provide access only for those individuals needing it to review. This strategy also helps prevent the need to create/rename existing accounts in staff turnover.

#3. Lock down your social media. Pay attention to online quizzes such as those on Facebook that ask things such as "Enter your mother's maiden name and birth year to see what your name was in your last life." Quizzes like this are made to harvest information and people often comment on them — those comments are made publicly available to all including those outside of your circle of followers. Go further on all your Instagram, Facebook, LinkedIn, Twitter, accounts, etc. and spend the time adjusting your privacy settings so that only your friends can see your personal information, pictures, friends list, etc.

Implement these MINIMUM safeguards

Recent headlines have alerted the public about the tens of millions of dollars paid to hackers around the world to remediate cyber attacks. Compromising systems has become very lucrative, so much so that hackers will now stop at nothing to compromise a business knowing that there is a big reward. It used to be that hackers would scan the internet themselves or use automated robots to find an open server or unpatched website. When they find one, they execute an attack using those vulnerabilities to compromise the system. When the hackers gain access, they execute tactics such as disabling and/or deleting system backups, downloading all the data and email databases, and then deploying ransomware. Your office computers are greeted with a pop-up saying your files are encrypted, how much you have to pay them to receive the decryption tool, an email address to correspond with the hackers, and a countdown timer telling you the price will increase if you don't act before it expires. In the early days of ransomware, restoring from an offsite or remote backup was sufficient to remediate the attack. The hackers have evolved their tactics and now show you screenshots of customer databases, personal information of patients, students, confidential shareholder agreements, tax returns and so forth.

Next, the hackers resort to blackmail, threatening to distribute this information directly to the affected parties, and that they will upload the records for sale on the dark web. This is the reason that large corporations are paying out and it's been insurance companies footing the bill. In response, governments and insurance companies are now pushing and advising to take an increased measure of cyber security no matter the size of the business. The following suggested safeguards are a small portion of what should be implemented in today's workplace but are no way the full spectrum of solutions available to fully safeguard your business.

a) First and foremost, 2FA/MFA (two-factor and multi-factor authentication) must be implemented in the most secure way. Simply put, MFA means a password is not the only security provision allowing access to accounts. The most common would be an SMS text message with a random six-digit code being sent to the account holder's phone after entering a password successfully. Unfortunately, the SMS method can be circumvented by hackers illegally porting out the mobile phone number. In response, many businesses are relying on using an authenticator app. Microsoft and Google have these: a QR code is presented which marries the application to the account. This can be configured in two ways: 1) a pop-up to approve or deny the sign-in attempt can be selected on the app. 2) the application will generate a six-digit code that expires and changes every minute that the sign-on prompt is open before a successful password has been entered. The latter six-digit method is advisable, as if staff have mistakenly hit "approve" when a password was compromised, the threat actor will gain entry to the account. It's unlikely a hacker will ever have access to see both the six-digit code from the authenticator app AND have the correct password.

b) Use next gen endpoint security – traditional antivirus won't cover you anymore. Use the analogy of "America's Most Wanted." If the faces of the now-biggest felons haven't been publicized, how are we to know who/what to look for? This is traditional antivirus; it recognizes only known threats. Traditional antivirus companies would have to have the virus reported to them, and then release an update; then the workstation or server would have to download that update. A virus released today trumps this system. This is called "0day" or "zero-day."

Next gen antivirus uses AI (artificial intelligence) and watches software behavior. If a file tries to connect to an outside server (in this case, a tool installed by a hacker) or it tries to change many files that haven't been accessed in years, it will stop the program from running. This has been effective with modern ransomware attacks. There are several security products that can be installed on workstations and servers that work in unison; a layered approach to endpoint security is the favorable provision for preventing hacks on the devices we use.

c) Email Protection – Phishing/Attachment filters – Phishing (as explained above) has gotten more complicated now where hackers are creating domains to bypass phishing scanners. For example, user@company.com receives an email from president@compamy.com. Notice the different spelling by replacing "n" with "m" in "company." Hackers will create domains similar to the target business domain name so the sending name passes these checks. Advanced phishing filters use AI to determine if these messages are from newly-created domains, if they are spoofing credible online retailers, and they will check for a history of interactions with a company. These filters also detect if the names match key employee names (controller's and CEO's) that come from outside of the company and if so, they will automatically be blocked. An additional provision is placing a visible banner advising the email came from the outside to keep staff on guard. It's still possible some illegitimate messages may bypass these filters, but a great number will be blocked, lessening the potential for a successful phish.

d) Use a password manager — Don't leave a spreadsheet or document saved in a convenient location called "Passwords" or "Logons." This is easy low-hanging fruit for hackers. Password protection of these documents is easily bypassed, as is extracting saved passwords from an internet browser. Use a manager like Keeper or 1password as it saves the passwords as encrypted which are inaccessible by a 3rd party (or even your IT team). Of course, protect these managers with 2FA.

e) Disable legacy remote access methods — Windows XP introduced and included a very convenient tool, Remote Desktop Protocol

(RDP). This was great for corporations and personal users because by opening the firewall on port 3389 you could access your computer from anywhere in the world as if you were sitting in front of it. Unfortunately, it lacked security and hackers quickly started utilizing this method to break into computers. In today's workspace, port 3389 should remain closed and RDP should NOT be used. If you want to challenge this theory, set up a test machine, open port 3389, and watch the hundreds of hunt attempts per hour for it. It is the simplest way for hackers to compromise a system and insurance companies tell tales of this being a leading cause of ransomware attacks compromising business networks.

f) Internal Policies — For your business and your employees, enforce the following of the practices outlined in this book. Generate a culture of being cyber risk aware.

Delegate and Educate

There is so much to be accounted for when protecting your business from cyber threats. IT has evolved so fast. Do you remember what cellphones looked like 15 years ago? What will cyber terrorism look like 15 years in the future? Computers are evolving and getting faster, AI is evolving, and hackers are keeping up and using new technologies to their benefit. It's equally important to maintain your cyber defense strategy on an ongoing basis. Like hiring security guards to watch your property around the clock, a leading IT expert will continually train and adapt the security monitoring protocols and monitoring technology. The same ideology should be applied to a cyber defense solution.

A competent firm will routinely train employees and vendors with the best current practices to maintain confidential information and safeguard access points into the corporate network. Tools will be coming out on an ongoing basis. The best endpoint security product today may not be the best tomorrow.

A 24/7/365 monitoring operation to watch for potential intruders is paramount and it's getting easier to access firms that offer a human team watching for threats around the clock as the demand grows.

There is immense value in having a 3rd party firm work alongside your existing IT team or internal IT administrator. The quick evolution of technology and the cyber threat landscape isn't something that can be kept up with alone — especially when maintaining all the responsibilities or growing a profitable business. Find a trusted cyber security IT firm and delegate the monitoring and implementation of the tools for your business. Have that firm, or an additional securities focused firm, perform regular checks based on new, evolving threats.

About the Author

Raised in Calgary Alberta Canada, Andrew Baker adopted an aptitude for Computers and IT as a teenager. In the early 90s, after being introduced to his first computer and then the inter-connectivity of local multi user chat rooms, he became fascinated with the intrigue of "how".

At the dawn of broadband internet, he launched his own online gaming service from his bedroom while living with his parents. The hosts of a competing online service nearly succeeded in hacking his system during an attempted malicious competitive take down. This spawned an intense vengeance driven crash course in cyber espionage where he not only swiftly learned how to exploit the vulnerabilities of offending online systems, he also learned how to protect them.

Fast forward to present day and Andrew is the owner of a thriving IT Management and Cyber Security Services business in his hometown. Cyber protection has always been at the forefront of his mind in conjuring ways that networks could fall vulnerable where corners are cut. He then adopts prevention practices and vowing never to let his clients' networks fall victim to an otherwise preventable incident.

Andrew is an avid snowboarder, traveler, camper and outdoors lover that spends time away from cities for days at a time without connectivity to the outside world. Through his business, he offers confidence in the security and stability of the networks he supports so that he and the staff of his customers can rest easy and focus on the life experiences that truly matter.

Andrew Baker

Technical Lead

IT Done Right

andrew@doingitright.ca

office: 403.456.5523

Protecting Your Business - Learn the Steps to Reducing Your Risk

By Peter Zendzian

Wow, congratulations, you made it this far. Impressive and no small accomplishment. But let me save you a little time. This chapter is one you may want to save yourself time and frustration and just pass over. Don't waste your time reading this chapter.

With all of the risks we have running our businesses, I'm sure you don't need to read a book that can make the simple act of reading your email become scary and frustrating. You already have to worry about your clients, employees, paying bills, balancing your checkbook, the government, and more. I'm going to save you a ton of time. Don't go any further and waste your time reading this chapter.

Wait, are you still reading? Was my warning not dire enough? Did I not convey my message well? I must not have, as I fear you will only cause yourself pain and anguish by continuing. The preceding and following chapters are infinitely more enjoyable and informative. Just remember, I did warn you.

As a child, I remember being told, "It's lonely at the top." On the top of the world and lonely. I didn't get it. As I grew older and started earning my own money, I would look at those in leadership roles, positions of authority and power, and think to myself they have it all and can do whatever they want. I know you sit there thinking to yourself how naive I was as a young man. Well, fellow entrepreneur, I can tell you with total understanding now. The top is lonely and scary. Even with loved ones, employees, and trusted advisors, you are alone to be accountable for your decisions. No one is coming. No one is coming to take responsibility. No one is coming to make the top any easier or less lonely. Even when your mountain is small, it is still as lonely as a tall mountain when you are on top. Those looking up to you will wonder, as I did, how much you have and how great it is to be where you are. Peer groups, mastermind groups, business socials, confer-ences, and other events may distract from the gravity of what it means to be the one accountable for every action, decision, and failure of your business. But they never remove the loneliness of being on the top.

Since you made it through that last part, I think you deserve to know a little secret. I understand why you're here. Well, I mean, it's not a secret. This is a book about business risk. You're here to learn about how to protect your business from the danger it faces. Every moment of every day, your business is at stake. Before you go any further, get a copy of this book, give it to another business owner. Have them read it and pass it on. Then discuss what you learn here.

Your business is in the business of making money, and we both know business money is not the same as personal money. Small businesses move vast sums of money. Small businesses make up nearly half of the United States economy.[17] That sort of means that the other half is big business. The significant difference between small businesses and your larger counter-parts is that the latter can more easily afford the tools and resources to fight and defend against the thieves working to steal your money. And there are people and organizations out there with complete freedom to do everything they can to steal that money. And they are really, really good at it.

According to the Cognyte CTI Research Group, the number of ransomware attacks nearly doubled in the first half of 2021. The 2020 CTI report found that 1,112 ransomware attacks involving data theft and data leakage occurred during the entire year. Compare that with the nearly 1,100 organizations that were victimized by ransomware in the first half of 2021. Those numbers are based on cases that were documented. Many cyber crimes go undocumented or don't make it into the more prominent news cycle,

---

[17] https://advocacy.sba.gov/2019/01/30/small-businesses-generate-44-percent-of-u-s-economic-activity

so there are more successful cyber attacks than we know about.

Ransomware is one of the top methods used by hackers to steal from businesses. According to the US Government's Cybersecurity and Infrastructure Assurance Agency (CISA):

Ransomware is an ever-evolving form of malware designed to encrypt files on a device, rendering any files and the systems that rely on them unusable. Malicious actors then demand ransom in exchange for decryption. Ransomware actors often target and threaten to sell or leak exfiltrated data or authentication information if the ransom is not paid.

So what does that mean?

Hackers take advantage of weak security spots to steal sensitive data or lock files. These criminals will only give you the key to access your system, or return the files, once you've paid their ransom. Remember the difference between big and small businesses... small businesses have more people doing multiple jobs, less secure networks, and fewer resources to stop attacks. It's almost as if they have no idea how easy of a target they are.

Things have changed, and they are not changing back. In the first half of 2021, we've already seen many high-profile attacks on organizations across America and the world. Only six ransomware gangs are responsible for the breach of cyber security defenses of 292 organizations. According to the eSentire Ransomware

Report, these criminals have so far stolen more than $45 million in ransom from their victims. You may recognize some of the following names:

- Colonial Pipeline: $4.4 million
- Brenntag chemical distribution: $4.4 million
- Acer Computer: $50 million
- JBS Foods: $11 million
- Quanta: $50 million
- National Basketball Association (NBA)
- AXA
- CNA - $40 million
- Cd Projekt (Refused to pay, they had comprehensive backups)
- Kia Motors - $20 million
- Buffalo public schools (Refused to pay but invested $10 million in infrastructure upgrades)

You may already be a victim of a cyber attack!

The cyber attack network is vast and has many players in multiple countries. It is very complex; one criminal network often rents out its software and networks to other smaller criminal organizations. Just think of it. Criminals are making a successful business of providing other criminals with the tools to attack and steal from your company.

Organizations of all sizes have been victims of cyber attacks. If your business is connected to the internet, there is a good chance it is already compromised. Any computer or device connected to a network where businesses interact online to pay suppliers, search the internet, email customers, etc. can be attacked by hackers.

According to a TechJury article from October 2021, 64% of businesses have experienced cyber attacks in the last 12 months.[18]

If that statistic doesn't scare you, here are a few more:

- 30,000 websites are hacked daily
- There were 20 million breached records as of March 2021
- Ransomware cases grew by 150% in 2020
- Email is responsible for more than 92% of all malware
- Every 39 seconds, there is a new attack somewhere on the web
- An average of around 24,000 malicious mobile apps are blocked daily on the internet
- 300,000 new pieces of malware are created daily

And here you are, a hard-working small business owner, striving to earn a living for you and your employees, working long days, foregoing vacations, and struggling through the most significant economic crisis of our time. All the while, professional criminals are doing everything they can to steal from you. Oh, and that insurance your insurance agent sold you, you know the cyber insurance policy... did you

---

[18] https://techjury.net/blog/how-many-cyber-attacks-per-day

read the fine print, the little details? There is a real possibility that should you become a victim of a cyber attack, that insurance policy you have to protect you from that same financial loss may not cover you. Yup, let me say that again. There is a good chance your insurance policy may not cover your losses from a cyber attack.

Insurance companies, like any business, are in the business of making money, and they are good at it. But over the last few years, cyber policies have gotten more and more expensive for them. Remember the statistics above? I can tell you with complete confidence that the insurance companies know those numbers, and more. There are minor caveats in those cyber policies now that expect you to have good cyber hygiene, proper cyber security and such. The policies throw around words like SIEM, EDR, XDR, and other abbreviations that change to keep up with the technology of cyber criminals. Think of health insurance and how they have dealt with pre-existing conditions. It's about the money. You have it, and everyone wants a little piece of it.

Do you remember my warning you to skip this chapter? I'm sorry you had to go through all of that. The internet is a dangerous, unforgiving wilderness, and it contains so many threats and predators. Sugarcoating the problem won't make it go away, and the only way I believe we can combat this crisis is to know our enemy, know their motivations, and meet them head-on. But there is a fatal flaw to my method here. We are fighting nation-states, anonymous faceless crime syndicates, organizations hiding behind corrupt governments, and the criminal hacking industry is exploding just like any other growth industry. And we as small business owners do not have the ability to go to battle with these organizations. We lack the resources, financial and moral. Our governments are limited by their ability to attack them or even protect themselves.

So what can you do?

If I had a nickel… yup, a nickel for every time I sat down with a business owner, laid out the risk they face, show the facts and what is needed to protect their business only to hear, "If I get hacked, I will just close the doors and go out of business." Yup, let Rome burn. But is that an option? Is it? Besides the pain of losing a business, think of the financial risk from "gross negligence." Because that is the exact phrase used in court when a company is destroyed when we don't protect it.

Let me ask again. What can you do?

To start, you must thoroughly inspect your systems for threats and vulnerabilities on an ongoing basis. Keep your network infrastructure up to date, licenses, and firmware constantly updated. Patch vulnerabilities quickly and put tools in place to protect your network from attack. At a minimum, this is a good start, but as Napoleon Hill says in *Think and Grow Rich*, you are stopping at "3 feet from gold." If you have not read the book or know the story, it's pretty simple. The analogy comes from a story of a young man during the gold rush. After mining for months, he gives up, and quits only three feet from the gold. Only in your case, your gold isn't just three feet away, it is just sitting there waiting to be stolen. The junk dealer who found the gold after the young man gave up didn't just start digging to find the gold. He hired an expert to guide him to the gold. And yup, it was only three feet further.

So, the same question? What can you do?

Many businesses don't understand their vulnerabilities and are not prepared to manage cyber attacks. And are you, indeed, any different? Fortunately, today, there are professional service providers who have the tools, experience, and resources to help identify and mitigate cyber risk vulnerabilities and help protect your business. You can read and study all you want and try to do it yourself... yet still only be three feet from the gold.

So, what can you do? I think the answer is pretty obvious now. Hire an expert. Isn't that why your clients hire you?

About the Author

Peter Zendzian is President of ZZ Servers, the company he co-founded in 2006. He leads a strong team of service-focused experts adept at designing, building, managing and maintaining secure information technology infrastructures that meet PCI, DFARS, NIST, HIPAA and Sarbanes-Oxley compliance.

A motivated and personable professional, Peter promotes teamwork and a family spirit at ZZ Servers – fostering a can-do attitude that clients trust.

Prior to launching ZZ Servers, Peter spent two decades in the U.S. Navy, retiring as Chief Petty Officer in 2009. There, he held a number of leadership roles spanning technology, training and project management. Peter also served as an Electronics Technician at General Dynamics Information Technology after his naval career.

Peter attended the College of Charleston before earning an Associate of Science degree in Electronics Engineering from Tidewater Community College.

Over the years, Peter has demonstrated a talent for quickly understanding and mastering technology, and he is accustomed to handling highly confidential records and documents – experience which has become core to the ZZ Servers offering.

Peter currently lives in Virginia Beach, Virginia.

Peter can be reached through his website: https://it-services.com.

Six Reasons Why Your Business Should Conduct Regular Security Assessments

By Joseph Salazar

Did you know that in 2021 every 11 seconds, a new organization will fall victim to ransomware?[19]

Artificial intelligence and machine language-based cyber security solutions are transforming everyday work life around the globe. Large-, medium- and small-sized businesses are bound to implement these programs to improve user experience, company productivity, and increase revenue. However, it has proved to be a double-edged sword when it comes to security and compliance. These solutions jeopardize the security of valuable data and infrastructure of the

---

[19] https://go.veeam.com/modern-applications-protect-from-ransomware.html

business at the hands of cyber security threats and cyber attacks.

Recent technological advancements are serving as a sleeve for critical hacks and breaches, making it difficult to track, detect, or mitigate them. In other words, a small gap in your security layer can leave your assets vulnerable to AI misuse, phishing scams, website spoofing, ransomware, malware, and IoT hacking. Did you know that the average cost of a single data breach is nearly $4 million USD? A prospering corporate executive like you can't afford this to happen. This leads us to a simple question: Are you prepared to protect your company from cyber security threats? How much can you tackle this dark side of digitization? If you think your current IT provider can save you with cyber security protection measures such as antivirus, backup, or firewall, then you are delusional. Wake up!

This is where regular security assessments can become your armor against cyber risks.

What is Cyber Risk?

The potential for an unexpected business failure to happen due to system or IT failure is called cyber risk. If you fear the theft of sensitive or regulated information, damage to the company's credentials, hardware, and consequent loss of data due to malware and viruses, the company's website, or damage to servers due to natural disasters, it means your company is at cyber risk.

It is important to understand the extent of the specific financial damages that an organization has to bear due to cyber risks. These include legal fees, downtime, and related loss due to customer distrust. This is just the beginning. In the worst-case scenario, you would end up submitting all your company records to the FBI, and this cycle would exhaust you.

What is a Security Assessment?

Cyber risk assessment is carried out to analyze and evaluate the availability, confidentiality, and integrity of valuable data, and assets of an organization. It identifies the internal and external threats as well as potential impacts of such threats upon suffering a cyber security incident. Conducting a comprehensive IT security assessment regularly gives you an edge in identifying and filling gaps in your security system, choosing appropriate protocols, evaluating potential security partners, establishing and maintaining compliance, and protecting essential data before you fall into the cyber trap.

Four Components and a Formula for IT Risk Assessment

You need the following four key components to assess IT risk. Let's move forward one by one:

- **Threat:** A threat is an event that could harm an organization's employees or property (such as natural disasters, website breakdowns, and corporate espionage).

- **Vulnerability:** A vulnerability is any potential liability that could cause damage to a threat — such as outdated antivirus software — that can become the gateway for a successful malware attack or server room location breach, or entry point for dissatisfied employees.

- **Impact:** Impact is the total damage an organization would suffer if the vulnerability is exploited by a threat, such as a successful ransomware attack. This can result in not only the loss of data and productivity but also the disclosure of customer data or trade secrets, resulting in loss of business, added legal fees, and penalties for non-compliance, as well as recovery cost.

- **Probability:** Possibility for any threat to occur is probability.

Why Do You Need Regular Security Assessments?

Here is why you need a comprehensive security assessment as soon as possible.

1. **Ensuring data security externally and internally**

The first thing we have been repeating throughout this chapter is data security. Every organization creates, receives, maintains, and transmits data that must be secured and protected. All data-storing platforms such as databases, servers, connected equipment, mobile devices, and cloud storage must be regulated and evaluated on a daily basis to monitor suspicious activity. This step is very important when your company has been offering new openings every month or has been terminating employees. The attacker can be anyone from a properly organized group to an ex-employee seeking revenge. This is why you have to keep an eye on data if it was moved, removed, or copied to other devices.

2. Identifying gaps in your cyber security layers

Security threats can be both external and internal (a hacker or an angry employee) or malware that may have entered your system searching for important information. Due to the COVID-19 pandemic and work-from-home, according to CBS news, cyber crime has gone up around 600%. Hackers have been developing sophisticated schemes for cyber crime and phishing emails, as per recent reports.

On July 2, 2021, one of the greatest ransomware crimes in history occurred. Kaseya, a global IT infrastructure provider, reportedly suffered an attack that used virtual system administrator (VSA) software to deliver REvil ransomware via automatic update. Here is what you need to know to understand the impact and scope of the Kaseya ransomware attack: Some Kaseya customers have managed service providers (SMEs) who have a contract to manage IT operations for thousands of other organizations. Threaten participants with REvil ransomware that exploits vulnerabilities to hack VSA software. VSA spreads REvil ransomware threats to its customers through SMBs. Thousands of organizations directly or indirectly involved in Kaseya became infected with the REvil ransomware.

People who learn from others' mistakes are smart. Regular security assessments help you to discover vulnerabilities and security risks associated with your entire IT environment. An organization can establish its line of defense with the tools and resources necessary to defend against external attacks, as long as the organization is aware of their vulnerabilities.

The security assessment will also include a classification of identified vulnerabilities based on the severity of the impact and guidelines for remediation. The purpose of a regular security assessment is to find out the hidden vulnerabilities, loopholes, and potential gaps in your company's security layers. Security assessments can help your system assess whether the security measures implemented adequately protect sensitive data from all potential attacks. Numerous service options are available, including internal and external penetration testing, database security assessments, and web application testing.

3. Improving network strength

A full assessment of your current IT or technical department is also incredibly important. A comprehensive and holistic view of your company's security strengths allows us to find the best solutions to improve and strengthen them like never before. Data breaches can cause significant losses to an organization, lead to legal problems, financial losses, and damage the company's image. Not all companies can recover.

Therefore, it does not harm the implementation of robust policies and procedures to strengthen the overall security of your organization. To do this effectively, start with a strategic security assessment and have it reviewed by industry experts.

In general, cyber security policies and procedures cover guidelines to manage control, dictate user account management, strengthen information security, and provide standards to improve the safety of workplaces and devices. A business continuity plan, disaster recovery plan, or other corrective actions, as well as security architecture and design assist with focusing on the appropriate implementation of IT systems and security controls.

The REvil cyber attack was first discovered on December 23, and Accellion originally claimed that the FTA vulnerability had been fixed within 72 hours, before being forced to explain that new vulnerabilities had been discovered. Another (and final) update to Accellion came in March, when the company claimed that all known vulnerabilities in the FTA, which authorities say were exploited by FIN11 and the Clop ransomware gang, had been fixed.[20]

However, respondents said Accellion's response to the incident was not as smooth as the company claimed. The documents were encrypted according to the company, but in a letter sent to those affected, the hackers had also obtained a decryption key. This event proves how important it is to conduct a regular security assessment.

4. Identifying training needs

IT software company Ivanti, which acquired Pulse Secure late last year, confirmed that attackers used Pulse Connect Secure (PCS) to target a limited number of customers. The three known shortcomings include CVE-2020-8243, CVE-2020-8260, and CVE-2019-11510, which CISA recently warned are among several CVEs attacked by the Russian Foreign Intelligence Service (SVR) in its efforts to target the United States. All of these vulnerabilities were fixed in 2019 and 2020 as per the company's statement. However, CVE-2021-22893, a new variant, was discovered recently. It is an authentication bypass vulnerability that could allow an unauthenticated attacker to execute arbitrary file execution on the Pulse Connect secure gateway.

Until you run a security assessment, you may not know what resources your business is using or abusing. For

---

[20] https://techcrunch.com/2021/07/08/the-accellion-data-breach-continues-to-get-messier

identified vulnerabilities, the security assessment identifies and helps prioritize the resources needed. On the other hand, with auditing, security assessments also help limit the resources and tools your business doesn't need but still pays for. This reduces unnecessary expenses and frees up the IT budget to invest in other critical aspects. In addition, a safety assessment also provides a platform for identifying employee training needs.

The gaps between employee training and operations, and company standards can be effectively identified and bridged with training and skills-development strategies.

5. Meeting Compliance Requirements

All organizations should demonstrate and document regular vulnerability checks to assess vulnerabilities, exploits, and vulnerabilities in office equipment, applications, and networks. Each entity should assess the likelihood and impact of potential risks, and implement and document appropriate safety measures to address those risk areas.

Security assessments vary in complexity and methodology. Your organization can choose from a range of services tailored to your needs, including vulnerability scanning, penetration testing, social engineering, database assessment, wireless testing, web application testing, and more. Documenting all security and privacy policies during the assessment will serve as an essential reference for procedural audits and as an excellent basis for staff training. However, with today's advanced hacking and cyber attack methods, compliance does not guarantee security. Regular (at least annual) assessments ensure that your organization identifies areas beyond compliance that need to be addressed to meet cyber security best practices and standards.

6. Developing Contingency Plans

Another advantage of regular risk assessment is the opportunity to develop disaster recovery plans. No security assessment can be completed without a thorough security plan. We work with you to develop security goals that are synchronized with your ongoing goals as an organization, so you are prepared for cyber security success at every step. Whether your data is stored on-premises, in the cloud, or both, developing a strategic backup plan is an essential part of recovery from cyber attacks and an overall security plan. Whether your organization's data is stored on-site, in the cloud, or both, a security assessment helps identify critical information that needs to be backed up. Start by prioritizing the company's most valuable assets; the main goal after a disaster is to resume primary business operations as soon as possible.

During the policy review, determine what information needs to be backed up and how to develop procedures for recovering backups after a failure, and standard procedures for regularly testing these recovery procedures. During any security disaster or breach, the organization must provide guidelines for recovering data and services from backups and other activities — a contingency plan developed through a security assessment.

The world's most valuable oil producer, Saudi Aramco, confirmed that the company's data leaked from one of its suppliers in early July, 2021. The files would now be used to extort $50 million. In May 2021, the Colonial Pipeline in the United States was hit by a ransomware cyber attack. In an emailed release, Aramco recently learned of indirect disclosure of a limited amount of corporate data held by third parties. The Saudi energy giant did not say which supplier was hit, or if the supplier was hacked, or if the files were otherwise disclosed. The AP report says the site offered data wiping in exchange for $50 million in cryptocurrency, though it's unclear who is behind the ransom. This isn't the first time Aramco has been the target of a data-related attack. In 2012, the company's computer network was hit by the Shamoon virus. If they had been vigilant enough to formulate a contingency plan with regular security assessments, then the company would never have made it to the news for this reason.

Prioritize Cyber Security Risks

At the end of the day, the goals are simple: safety and security. If you think that heading a small business can save you since there are other big fish in the market, then you are wrong. Don't risk your security at any cost. All cyber criminals need is your negligence and ignorance to hack the essential data out of your system while you are sleeping. It would be too late for regrets, if you fall prey to a cyber attack or get a ransom email demanding a million dollars. The chances are high that paying that amount as ransom won't even solve your issue.

Save yourself from losing your assets and getting extorted for your whole life. Regular cyber security audits are the ultimate solution to protect your data and money. We have been helping small- to medium-sized businesses in Orange County, California protect their computer networks since 1996, and we continue to evolve our solutions with the changing cyber attack landscape. A regular security assessment includes firewall security review, penetrating testing, vulner-ability scanning, risk, and a compliance assessment. Visit our website today to find out more about complete a cyber security assessment to protect your business from cyber attacks.

About the Author

Joseph Salazar is the Vice President of Operations at Netwiz Computers located in Placentia, California. He lives nearby in Yorba Linda, and has nearly 30 years of experience working in the IT industry. Starting out as a Helpdesk IT Support Technician, Joseph quickly climbed the ranks, gaining industry knowledge with every step he took, leading him to where he is today.

Joseph got into this field because he was fascinated by how important problem solving was in the IT industry and he noticed how solutions were constantly having to adapt to new threats. When several IT firms were hit with ransomware, he spent weeks working intensely with these firms, figuring out how they had been attacked and what they could do to ensure it didn't happen to his clients. He quickly realized it was not just important to find out what caused a cyberattack, but also to figure out how to prevent it from happening in the future. Each day brought a new threat and each day he brought a new solution.

In addition to his role at Netwiz Computers, Joseph also takes pride in being active in his community. He is an active member of the Yorba Linda Chamber of Commerce and is the President of the Brea Kiwanis Club. They do various fundraisers that help provide assistance to less fortunate kids in the area. His Kiwanis club also puts on the popular city-wide Spelling Bee, the Essay Contest as well as the Toys for Tots and Easter Egg Hunt providing toys and treats for the children. He also feeds the seniors at the Senior center as well as provides free services to wash their cars and mow their lawns.

As Vice President of Operations for Netwiz Computers, Joseph helps his company serve the Orange County area by providing reliable, consistent, and professional IT services. They have been successful at doing it since 1998. They focus on providing their clients with Enterprise-level services and solutions for small businesses. Time and experience have helped them develop best practices and workflow procedures around a proactive philosophy designed to minimize disruption and keep their clients focused on their business, not their technology.

You can connect with Joseph at:

NetwizComputers.com

joe@netwizcomputers.com

(714) 455-2925

Three Types of Cyber Security Breaches & How Your Business Can Minimize Risk

By Gregory Bledsoe

If YOUR company has a WEAK or LAXED POSTURE with regards to CYBER SECURITY and information technology systems, YOU are a hacker's dreams, and your company could be the next cyber crime victim. Chrysalis MSP is an industry managed IT leader with specializations in cyber security, Office 365, cloud solutions, and Voice Over IP (VoIP). The attempt with this book is teach, to educate, and to help business owners fight through their painful cyber security experiences and learn lessons from other business owners that have been victims of cyber crime. Over the years, my team and I have helped several businesses recover after experiencing a cyber crime or cyber attack and in almost every case we are asked, "What could we have done to prevent this from happening? Or how can we protect ourselves from something like this in the future?" Our response is always, "An ounce of prevention is worth a pound of cure." To which they typically respond, "We didn't think this could happen to us," or, "We thought we were protected." I want to share with you three different types of breaches and how they occurred and how you can minimize your risk and protect your business against cyber security's silent business-killer.

Scenario 1 — Engineering Firm: 35 users (Virus)

An end user (comptroller) received an email from a vendor demanding payment for an invoice that was 90 days past due. The email also included instructions to click a link in the body of the email to view and verify the amount in question. In this situation, the user clicked the link but because nothing happened, a call to the service desk was made seeking assistance with the broken link. While on the call, a new problem occurred, the user could no longer access any files on the company server and several other employees started reporting the same issue. Yes, you guessed it — the company had been hacked and everything was encrypted. A few minutes, later an email was received demanding a payment of 25% of the company's annual revenues within 72 hours and if not paid, access to the company data would be gone forever. The company in this scenario didn't pay the ransom because they had backups; however, it took six weeks to fully recover all systems, and during this time, with limited access to files and idle employees unable to work, several projects were late and losses were over $500K.

An "ounce of prevention." What could have prevented this experience?

TIP 1. Provide Cyber Security Awareness Training & Testing

Most business owners don't realize that internal employees are the biggest threat to a company when it comes to cyber security. Cyber security awareness training increases employees' awareness levels and give them the practical skills needed to better protect and recognize potential cyber threats via email. It is also vital to test employees frequently through phishing simulations to ensure that they are retaining what they learned and refreshing their knowledge when needed.

TIP 2. Update to Next Generation Antivirus

Traditional antivirus software just can't keep up. In 2019, according to the National Security Alliance, a new malware strain was discovered every 4.2 seconds. Next-generation antivirus solution protects and prevents known and unknown attacks, by monitoring, responding to attackers' tactics, techniques, and procedures.

TIP 3. Update Next Generation Firewall

A next generation firewall (NGFW) is hardware of software technology that is capable of detecting and blocking sophisticated attacks by enforcing security policies at the application, port, and protocol levels.

Scenario 2 — Personal Injury Law Firm: 25 users (Weak Password)

The user (Point of Contact - POC) calls the service desk, "Can your company help us? I can't access any files on the shared drive and all the files look like gibberish." Yes, you guessed it — this company had been hacked and everything was encrypted. A few moments later, everyone in the law firm received this example email and a link to a website with all the firm's confidential data viewable and unprotected:

Hello,

We have been in your system for some time, and we have copied all your data from the XXXXX server \ (we have attached several files as proof). If you do not pay us 5 BTC within 72 hours, we will publish this data in the public domain on the internet.

Attachment name:

LAW FIRM PASSWORDS.docx

An "ounce of prevention." What could have prevented this experience?

Tip 1. DO NOT SHARE Passwords

There is no security with an unencrypted shared password document.

Tip 2. Change ALL Passwords

Change all passwords and implement a password management system. Password management systems protect and store your login details in an encrypted vault, users no longer need to reuse the same password, which is one of the most common reasons why accounts get hacked.

Tip 3. Create Company Password Policies

Example:

- Strong passwords
- Must be at least 10 characters long
- Must contain different types of characters
- Must include upper/lowercase letters and numbers
- Must include special character

Scenario 3 — Healthcare Provider (Phishing)

The Practice Manager of an urgent care facility receives an email from Microsoft stating it's time to change the current Office 365 password. The user follows the instructions in the email and clicks the "change password" link. After trying several times, the user decides to give up because the link doesn't appear to be working. Later that day, the service desk receives a call from the practice manager asking for help because the email inbox was being inundated with hundreds and hundreds of spam emails, making it impossible to read legitimate emails. The practice manager explained that after deleting over 500 spam emails with no end in sight, they decided to call in the cavalry for help. The "change password" email was not from Microsoft — it was a phishing email used to trick the practice manager into entering the correct and current login credentials into a look-alike Office 365 webpage portal. While the user was busy deleting and being distracted by all the spam emails, they were unable to read or acknowledge legitimate emails being sent regarding all the credit card charges being made by the hacker.

An "ounce of prevention." What could have prevented this experience?

Tip 1. SET UP Multi-Factor Authentication (MFA)

MFA is an electronic authentication method in which a user is granted access to a website or application only after successfully presenting two or more pieces of evidence (or factors) to an authentication mechanism: knowledge (something only the user knows), possession (something only the user has), and inherence (something only the user is). MFA protects user data — which may include personal identification or financial assets — from being accessed by an unauthorized third party that may have been able to discover, for example, a single password.

Tip 2. Provide Cyber Security Awareness Training & Testing

Most business owners don't realize that internal employees are the biggest threat to a company when it comes to cyber security. Cyber security awareness training increases employees' awareness levels and gives them the practical skills needed to better protect and recognize potential cyber threats in emails. It is also vital to test employees frequently through phishing simulations to ensure that they are retaining what they learned and refreshing their knowledge if needed.

Tip 3. Internet & Web Content Filtering

Web content filtering helps fight against ransomware attacks by proactively blocking dangerous websites that could infect a user's machine with the ransomware software without their knowledge.

Cyber security attacks on small businesses are increasing and the business community must be proactive when protecting computer networks and systems. An ounce of prevention is worth a pound of cure — the tips previously mentioned can help you minimize the risk in your business from cyber criminals.

About the Author

Gregory Bledsoe is President and Chief Executive Officer of Chrysalis MSP, an Information Technology Company located in Houston, Texas. Gregory Bledsoe is a Summa Cum Ladue graduate of Capella University, where he received a BS in Information Technology. Bledsoe's passion for computers began at the age of 15 after a high school friend sold him a Commodore Vic-20 for fifty dollars.

Prior to Chrysalis MSP, Bledsoe spent 18 years in the corporate world, with roles at companies such as HL&P (Now NRG), Invesco, ExxonMobil, and Anadarko Petroleum before venturing out into world of entrepreneurship. Today, Bledsoe continues to help small and medium size businesses manage and tackle the challenges of Information Technology. Bledsoe also served in the United States Air force, and Texas National Guard from which he was Honorably Discharged in 1992.

Why Your Disaster Recovery Plan Could Save Your Business

By David Burton and Wes Jensen

Back in 2017, data displaced oil as the world's most valuable resource. It's easy to see why: Data powers virtually every decision in a business, from marketing tactics, to product development, to long-term direction and proactive strategy.

Therefore, it is imperative for all organizations to have a disaster recovery plan that protects their data. Disaster could mean anything from flooding and physical vandalism and theft, to cyber attacks and data breaches.

FEMA reports[21] that almost 40% of small businesses close permanently after a disaster. Data specialists, Nexstor, revealed these alarming statistics:[22]

---

[21] https://safetymanagement.eku.edu/blog/the-challenge-of-reopening-a-business-after-a-natural-disaster/
[22] https://nexstor.com/why-you-need-a-disaster-recovery-plan/

- Unplanned outages and downtimes costed businesses $926 per minute in 2016 (the cost is higher today).

- 90% of businesses without a disaster recovery plan will close following a major systems failure. Put differently, only 10% survive major failure.

- 60% of small businesses that lose their data will not survive six months.

- Only 10% of businesses without a disaster recovery plan will survive.

It is impossible to quantify the actual losses that a business suffers after a major failure/breach. Customers are unlikely to forgive data breaches, expecting businesses to handle their data with utmost security. Such a business would be looking at high customer defection, particularly if consumer data was affected.

However, putting together a comprehensive disaster recovery plan is no walk in the park. In this chapter, you will learn about the importance of a disaster recovery plan and what to think about when formulating and implementing your disaster recovery strategy.

What Is a Disaster Recovery Plan?

A disaster recovery plan/strategy is a collection of procedures, policies, and tools that a business can use to recover any disruption to its IT or data systems. Each business will have a tailored set of tools and procedures depending on your data, IT assets, and data recovery goals.

In this context, a "disaster" covers any event that disrupts access to IT systems, apps, or data. It includes corruption of data stores/centers, fires, power failures/outages, cyber attacks (malware, ransomware, data breaches, DDoS attacks), vandalism, theft, terrorism, or natural disasters like floods, earthquakes, or hurricanes, among others.

A disaster recovery plan aims to overcome the disaster and restore normal operations within the shortest possible time.

Components of a Disaster Recovery Plan

A comprehensive DR plan should incorporate strategies to recover from as many disastrous events as possible. At the minimum, it should outline the following:

- **Recovery Point Objectives (RPO)** – This is a measure of the amount of data that could be lost during recovery. Adjusting backup frequency controls this parameter.

- **Remote Data Backups (RDB)** – It is critical to maintain an offsite data backup to protect your most important data assets as part of your DR plan

- **Recovery Time Objectives (RTO)** – Estimate the time it takes to resume normal operations following a disastrous event. The RTO balances a business' resources and the need for business continuity. It takes more resources to implement a faster RTO.

- **DR Plan Testing** – All DR plans should be subjected to frequent simulation tests to ensure that the RPOs and RTOs are realistic, and the teams are prepared to face actual disasters.

- **Accountability Chart** – This chart outlines the persons/teams in charge of implementing various disaster recovery procedures. It outlines the roles and responsibilities of all players so that they can act quickly and enforce the plan consistently.

Some of the other details the plan should include are:

- Data backup and recovery solutions/processes/technologies

- Redundancy of equipment and hardware

- Secondary business locations

- Failover systems

All together, these components create a seamless workflow through all stages of the disaster management lifecycle: prevention, preparation, mitigation, and recovery. The disaster recovery plan must be well-documented. It should have detailed instructions on responses to various unplanned disruptions.

Organizations today can outsource their disaster recovery plan, known as Disaster Recovery as a Service (DRaaS). Today, organizations' disaster recovery needs are complex, as they must plan for much more significant amounts of data stored/accessed/created in hundreds, even thousands, of devices.

The Difference Between Disaster Recovery and Business Continuity Plans

It is easy to confuse disaster recovery and business continuity, given that both have the same goal. However, disaster recovery is a small part of an overall business continuity strategy.

Business continuity refers to measures taken to keep business operations running, despite interruptions. It encompasses strategies to keep running, for example, even while disaster recovery procedures are under-way.

Therefore, the DR plan has a more limited scope compared to the business continuity plan. It might not have contingency plans for all business processes, human resources, or business partners.

Importance of a Disaster Recovery Plan

Any disruption to the ongoing operations — and the resultant downtime — can significantly affect a business's profitability on multiple fronts. Each disastrous event — even the loss of just one business-critical file — can translate to losses amounting to thousands or even millions of dollars, depending on the company size.

Suppose your business falls victim to just one ransomware attack. Your files are encrypted, and entire systems are rendered unusable across the organization. This could go on for days, even weeks, if you didn't have backup data or a disaster recovery plan. Conversely, if you did, you could easily switch to your backup data files and keep running within a few hours.

The thing about IT failures, aside from nefarious attacks, is that they will happen at one point or other. It's a matter of **when** not **if**. Some common threats to business continuity include:

Cyber Attacks

In 2020, there were 1,001 cases of data breaches,[23] exposing or otherwise affecting the records of 155.8 million individuals in the US alone. Cyber attacks today have become even more sophisticated, and they can happen in thousands of ways.

Any organization can have thousands of vulnerable points in its IT and data systems, and it is nearly impossible to secure them all. For example, in the 2018

---

[23] https://www.statista.com/statistics/273550/data-breaches-recorded-in-the-united-states-by-number-of-breaches-and-records-exposed/

British Airways breach,[24] hackers simply injected an e-skimming code into the company website to change its behavior.

Malware and ransomware attacks aim to corrupt, encrypt or destroy your files. Some even try to wipe out entire mainframes. You must have a recovery plan against departmental or organization-wide breaches. Ninety-six percent of companies with comprehensive DR plans recover well from cyber attacks.

Natural Disasters

Most companies don't give enough credence to Mother Nature's potential influence on their IT systems. Since the 1970s, companies have endured systematically rising losses because of natural disasters. In 2017, for instance, there were 16 data loss events because of natural calamities costing the businesses over $1 billion.

It is important to have a plan for securing your data and IT assets should a natural disaster strike. With the imbalances caused by climate change, we'll see more incidences of wildfires, floods, tornadoes, hurricanes, and earthquakes.

Where is your business location relative to fault lines, flood plains, wind direction, and other dangers? In your DR plan, ensure that your secondary backup location is far from danger zones. Onsite data backups are of no use in the event of a flood or hurricane.

---

[24] https://www.bbc.com/news/uk-england-london-45440850

Acts of Terrorism

Research has shown[25] that acts of terrorism from 2000-2018 cost the global economy a jaw-dropping US$ 855 billion. That's more than enough money to run Turkey or the Netherlands for a year.[26]

Depending on your line of business and its location, your disaster recovery plan must include preparations for an attack on your business premises. More likely, however, you would make arrangements to cover for infrastructural damage or power disruptions resulting from terror acts near your business.

Hardware Failures and Power Outages

IT infrastructure will always be prone to hardware malfunctions for various reasons: human/user error, age, network breakdowns, accidents, power outages/surges, etc. It is critical to have a DR plan that outlines hardware maintenance protocols to avoid unnecessary device/ infrastructural failures.

However, there will be unprecedented failures which the business cannot control. In this case, you need a near-instant solution to sidestep the failure according to the stipulated RPO and RTO capabilities.

User Errors

People make mistakes; the more people, the higher the potential for data losses or system/hardware

---

[25] https://www.degruyter.com/document/doi/10.1515/peps-2020-0031/html
[26] https://www.worldometers.info/gdp/gdp-by-country/

failures resulting from those mistakes. The results could be catastrophic, from mundane issues like forgetting to save a file, to more serious ones like staff leaving themselves logged into the company system on a foreign device.

Because people are people, it is impossible to prevent these kinds of mistakes completely. However, you can institute checks and systems to decrease the likelihood of adverse outcomes. Your DR plan should include regular backups to create a series of system restore points to roll back to if a mistake occurs.

In this setup, you should consider your workforce and their level of expertise, then anticipate the kinds of errors they are likely to make. Logs from the IT support team can be very helpful here. Apart from continuous backups, you can increase staff training so that all users are aware of the latest security protocols and what to do when they make a mistake.

Six Steps For Creating a Comprehensive Data Recovery Plan

A comprehensive disaster recovery plan must consider the most likely disruptions an organization may face and plan procedures and tools for recovery. As mentioned earlier, there are hundreds of risk factors, and organizations' resources are typically limited based on their size.

Nevertheless, it is possible to optimize resources and DR planning to cover the organization in the event of the most likely and most catastrophic disasters. These are the steps to follow when creating a disaster recovery plan:

Step #1: Perform an IT Resource Audit

An IT resource audit is the process of naming and quantifying all the components of your IT system during normal operations. Essentially, you must establish a base level that defines "normal," which will be the target of your disaster recovery.

Understand the distinct data and IT resources you possess by creating an inventory. Mark what each resource holds and streamline each to ease backup and recovery should disaster strike.

Step #2: Define Your Mission-Critical Data Assets

Even the smallest business has hundreds of processes and generates large volumes of data every day. Not all data and processes are critical to business continuity; most data generated will be redundant or unimportant.

During your IT resource audit, you must decide which data sets are critical to your operations and which ones aren't. Otherwise, you will waste a lot of storage and processing power to back up non-essential data and end up slowing the very systems you're trying to preserve. During your audit, take time to organize your data and remove inessential files so that you optimize both storage and processor utility.

Step #3: Define Roles and Responsibilities

As mentioned, the accountability chart is a critical component of any disaster recovery plan. All employees in the business have a role to play within the DR plan. Even simple tasks like escalating potential cyber security threats can save entire systems from collapse at the moment of truth.

Define what each person's actions should be in the event of various types of disasters. They should know what to do and who to report to, and this information should be regularly tested so that they remain aware. Your DR plan is only as effective as its executors.

Step #4: Set Recovery Goals

Recovery goals include RTOs and RPOs — this is where you define how quickly you'd like the organization to recover from disastrous events. Here, you must define what and how much data you can afford to lose when disaster strikes (and what you can't).

Any effective data recovery plan should have realistic and specific recovery point and recovery time objectives. For instance, prioritize data recovery to begin with mission-critical data and system assets, working in decreasing order of priority. More important assets will be backed up more often and retrieved/recovered sooner after a disaster, while less important assets will be backed up less frequently and recovered later.

Mission-critical data — like financial data, compliance data, customer information, supply chain information — should have the most stringent RPOs and RTOs to minimize operational disruption. Depending on your operations, you may go so far as to run a parallel backup production server to take over from the normal server if disaster strikes.

Step #5: Get Remote Data Storage

Even if you run an onsite data center with data backups, you must store a backup in a remote location. Otherwise, you could lose your data forever if a natural disaster destroys your primary data store.

Natural disasters are not the only cause for concern; ransomware attacks have also crippled entire data stores and halted operations. Vandalism, theft, and physical tampering are other types of disasters that can affect both primary and backup stores in the same location (or general region).

With remote backups, you can simply purge the corrupted files and restore data from your backups. This is time consuming, of course, so you should look into ways of operating from the cloud so that you can restore operations before moving all the data back to your primary stores.

Today, most businesses should have a cloud-based, remote backup solution that can automatically download and copy data every day (or every few hours). Manual backup solutions like disks or tapes have fallen into disuse, but they can be helpful when you need to isolate your data from corrupted systems.

Since this is quite complicated and technical, it's best to outsource all your disaster recovery needs to a DRaaS vendor. Most of these providers have robust DR plans that include everything from simple backups to fully operational cloud environments that power business operations while the primary network is being fixed.

Step #6: Test Your Recovery Plan Regularly

Creating a disaster recovery plan is only the first step in protecting your business from disruptions. An effective DR plan is one that has been tested extensively and optimized to reflect the reality of your team's capabilities and potential hazards.

You must subject your DR plan to regular testing for two reasons: to reorient your team with their roles in light of various disasters, and to prove that the plan works for various disasters.

When creating your testing protocols, remember to think about:

Single points of failure

What are the systems that lack redundancy in the DR plan? Can you still implement your DR plan if these systems are attacked/fail/have a problem?

Recovery time

How long — from the start of your simulation — does it take to restore bare minimum operations? How long until normal operations resume? How can you decrease these recovery times?

Recovery point

How much data did you lose when switching from your primary data to the remote data? How much of the lost data was critical? By verifying recovery points, you can reduce the chances of losing mission-critical data during a real emergency.

Disaster type

Effective tests should be clear on the type of disaster simulation in question. For example, what would you do in the event of data corruption, or a natural disaster, or an external data breach?

Consider the different types of disasters that can happen and create testing protocols for them at different times. Repeat the most likely and cata-strophic scenarios during your regular drills (say, monthly or bimonthly). This way, your team will be ready for different disasters.

Regular testing will also help you know which areas of your DR plan need to be improved or updated, which increases your business' resiliency in the face of an actual disaster.

Summary: Don't Gamble with Your Organization's Most Valuable Asset

As you can see, neglecting a solid disaster recovery plan is simply not worth the risk to your business. It's not about losing money only; rather, it's about maintaining your customers' confidence, avoiding productivity hitches, and making the most of all business opportunities you find.

Your customers in this digital age expect nothing less than digital perfection. Even the biggest business will feel the pinch of losing customer confidence following a data breach. If you think customer acquisition is costly, try re-acquisition!

About the Authors

David Burton

After David Burton graduated with a civil/structural engineering degree, he was challenged with networking five departments together to improve business efficiencies.

Upon successful completion, he was asked to return to his previous role. "No, thank you!" he said.

David had discovered his passion. It was more than improved bottom-line numbers. There was a distinct positive buzz throughout the office. He quit his job, started technology consulting, and never looked back.

Two decades of cybersecurity experience and an MBA has taught David the value of leveraging a strategic approach to technology. David's approach helps clients achieve business resilience by planning for unforeseen events and implementing a framework to minimize downtime.

Wes Jensen

Before starting his first IT company in 2001, Wes was the network administrator at the largest K-8 school district in California. Being the only administrator, with the responsibility of managing over 50 locations and thousands of end-points, he learned to efficiently leverage technology management at scale.

When Wes was introduced to his first small business client, he realized that most companies are either struggling with needless inefficiencies with their computer systems, or even worse, operate in such a way that it puts the survival of the company at risk.

In 2019, David and Wes formed Cyber Security Advisors to enhance the services provided to their clients. Their vision for Cyber Security Advisors is to help businesses reduce their risk and become the most productive and protected in the US.

Interested in partnering with David, Wes, and the team at Cyber Security Advisors? Please contact them at www.CyberSecurityAdvisors.com.

Reduce Your Liability & Identify Your Business Risk

By John Hill

First, let's define risk. Risk is simply the concept of the likelihood of loss. The likelihood that the business is going to lose money. For instance, what is the risk of a computer shutting down and how much money will that cost the business? Remember, this is both a business problem and a technology problem so you have to determine what implication the risk has for the business and the return on investment for the remediation of risks. Will it cost more to remediate a risk than the value of what's being protected?

As a business owner, you have a huge responsibility for every aspect of your business, so the decisions and actions you take every day will either put your business at risk and give you greater liability, or reduce your risk and reduce your liability. But you might ask, "What does that really mean for myself and my business? How do I identify my risks and how do I reduce them?"

I recently spoke with the owner of a company that expressed a concern about their finance officer that just left the company under less-than-friendly circumstances. The owner was concerned that the ex-employee might still have access to some of their online and in-house systems. He said that she also managed their Microsoft 365 email and their server and that she didn't give him all the administrator passwords when she left. He asked me if I could help him, so I scheduled a meeting with him to review what he knew about his online and local systems for the next day.

Myself and one of my team members met with him and began interviewing him and his team to gather as much information as possible about his systems so we could conduct a cyber security risk assessment for him. We gathered the administrative passwords he knew, made an inventory of his computer and network assets, and got a list of his employees. With that information in hand, we set up several different scans of his network to collect information over a period of several days to give ourselves and our client a better idea of the issues he had but was unaware of.

As a managed information technology and cyber security solutions provider, our team at TechSage Solutions has the opportunity to assist many small- to mid-sized companies with business risk assessments and assist with solutions to reduce the risk threat. Our team is skilled at assisting with the resolutions for the type of scenario described above.

As business owners, you have an obligation to yourself, your employees, and your clients to identify your business risks, determine what your liability might be as a result of those risks, and take proactive steps to reduce them. You might ask, "Why should this be important to me? Why should I devote time and effort to this? My business isn't at risk, we're small, we don't have much important data, no one would want to hack us. Our office is in a very safe location so we don't have to worry about break-ins or theft of our records or our computer systems."

If believe any of these things, unfortunately you are wrong, and you are putting your business at risk. The statistics found in the "Fundera Small Business Cybersecurity Statistics" report for this year, 2021, should concern you. Here's 28 of the most important things you should know.

Cyber Security Statistics[27]

1. 43% of cyber attacks target small businesses.

2. 60% of small businesses that are victims of a cyber attack go out of business within six months.

3. Cyber crime costs small and medium businesses more than $2.2 million a year.

4. There was a 424% increase in new small business cyber breaches last year.

---

[27] 30 Surprising Small Business Cyber Security Statistics (2021), https://www.fundera.com/resources/small-business-cyber-security-statistics, October 6, 2021

5. 66% of small businesses are concerned or extremely concerned about cyber security risk.

6. 14% of small businesses rate their ability to mitigate cyber risks and attacks as highly effective.

7. 47% of small businesses have no understanding of how to protect themselves against cyber attacks.

8. 66% of small businesses are most concerned about compromising customer data.

9. 3 out of 4 small businesses say they don't have the personnel to address IT security.

10. 22% of small businesses encrypt their databases.

11. Human error and system failure account for 52% of data security breaches.

12. 63% of confirmed data breaches leverage a weak, default, or stolen password.

13. Cyber attacks caused by compromised employee passwords cost $383,365 on average.

14. 1 in 323 emails sent to small businesses are malicious.

15. The median small business received 94% of its detected malware by email.

16. 54% of small businesses think they're too small for a cyber attack.

17. 25% of small businesses didn't realize cyber attacks would cost them money.

18. 83% of small businesses haven't put cash aside for dealing with a cyber attack.

19. 54% of small businesses don't have a plan in place for reacting to cyber attacks.

20. 65% of small businesses have failed to act following a cyber security incident.

21. 50% of small and mid-sized businesses reported suffering at least one cyber attack in the last year.

22. Small businesses spend an average of $955,429 to restore normal business in the wake of successful attacks.

23. Just figuring out how a cyber attack happened could cost $15,000.

24. 40% of small businesses experienced eight or more hours of downtime due to a cyber breach.

25. This downtime accounts for an average of $1.56 million in losses.

26. Cyber attacks are projected to cause $6 trillion in damages by 2021.

27. Industry experts say a small business' cyber security budget should be at least 3% of a company's total spending.

28. 91% of small businesses don't have cyber liability insurance.

As a small- to mid-sized business owner or manager, you should read through this list several times and understand that you have substantial risk unless you take action to avoid or at least reduce it. Based on the risk factors shown above, you now need to accomplish a cyber security risk review and analysis to determine what course of action you must take to reduce the liability as well as potential liability you could face if you don't do anything about it.

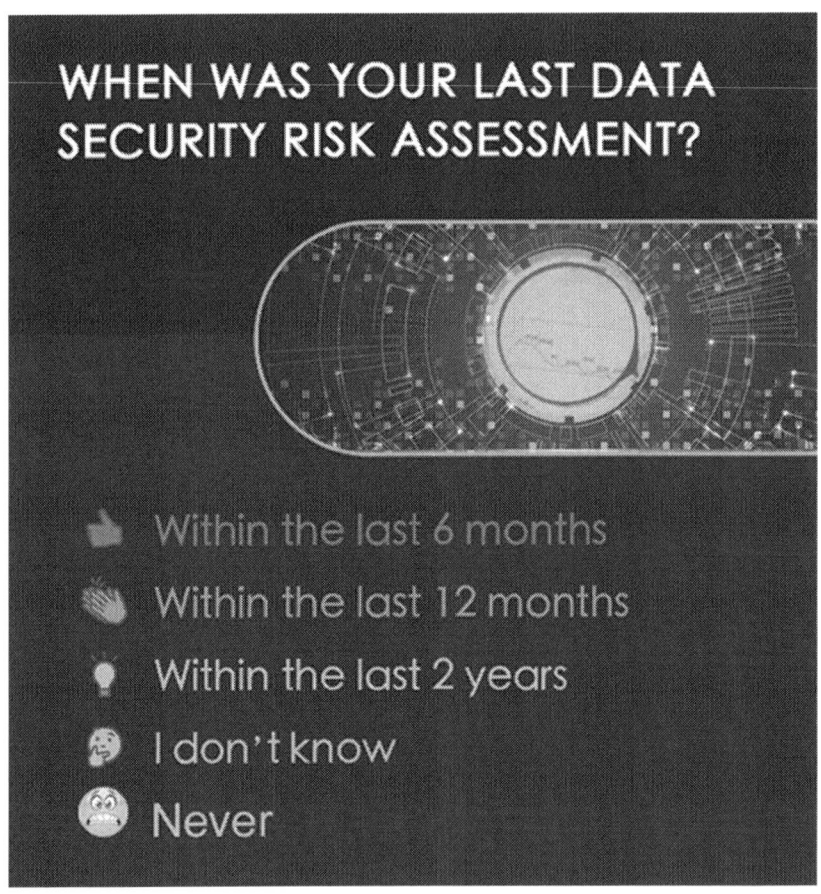

Reproduced with permission from Kaseya.

General Business Risk

While the focus of this book is on cyber security risks and the importance of assessing those risks, let's briefly broaden the scope of our discussion from our focus on cyber security risk to the wider overall scope of business risk. We can include the actual IT equipment you may have that is at risk. This can include things like servers, desktops, laptops, printers, phones, cabling, cabinets, and media. We can broaden the discussion even more by including infrastructure like buildings, cabinets, furniture, and safes. To round it out, let's include outsourcing like power equipment, communications equipment, and even consultants.

You're probably thinking to yourself, "What are some of the things that impact this larger scope of business risks?" The short answer is, a lot. You can experience application errors or accidental changes of information, the dreaded user errors, physical threats like bomb attacks or threats, vandalism, or even terrorism. You can have contract breaches, natural disasters such as floods, fire, tornadoes, earthquakes, or lightning strikes. How about destruction of records or deterioration of physical media, theft, fraud or embezzlement, equipment failure or unauthorized access to your information technology like proprietary documents or network diagrams? This list could go on and on but I think you get the idea.

Since you now have an idea of what some of your business risks are, what can you do about it? First, you have to narrow down the list to the things that are most important to you. Another way to put it is, what are the unacceptable risks you need to focus on? Once you've decided on the risks that are important to focus on, there are four options to consider when mitigating them. You can just accept the risk, avoid the risk, transfer the risk, or if possible, apply the appropriate security controls. For instance, if you determine that the other options are too costly in time, effort or actual dollars, you may decide to just accept the risk and move on.

Here's a graphical representation of how threats, plus vulnerability, plus impact results in your level of risk and how each component contributes to the level of risk.

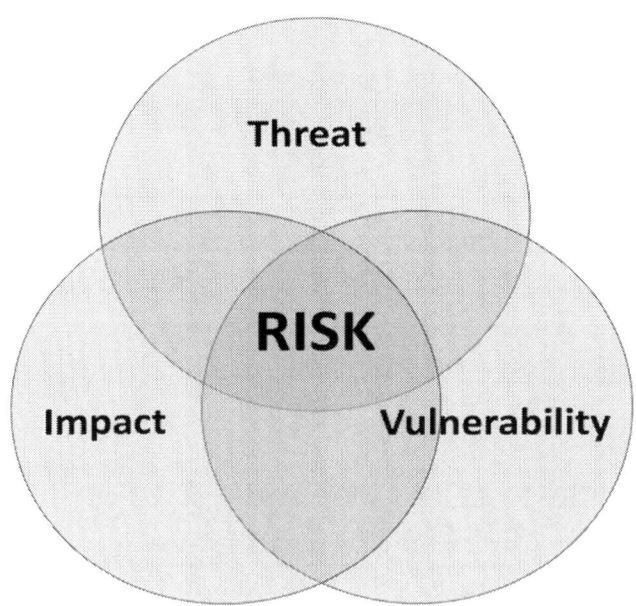

Using the process described in the last paragraph, you can accomplish a risk analysis on each of the potential business risks you're facing to determine how you can effectively reduce your liability while maintaining or growing your business. Now, let's break down your risk analysis into some more detailed steps:

- Evaluate the likelihood and impact of potential risks
- Assign ownership of the risk to a team member
- Implement appropriate security measures to address the risks identified in your risk analysis
- Document the chosen security measures, and, where required, the rationale for adopting those measures
- Maintain continuous, reasonable, and appropriate security protections

I hope this brief discussion about business risks has given you a basic understanding about what a risk assessment is and why it's critical to your business to review your business risks — both cyber and physical — on a regular basis. When things change in your business, it's important to review any risks that might come with the change and determine if you can just accept the risk or if you need to take action to reduce or eliminate the risk.

As a measure to increase your awareness of what's going on in the cyber security arena that could affect your business, I invite you to sign up for our FREE weekly cyber security tips today for yourself and your employees at https://www.techsagesolutions.com/Securitytips.

Plus, if you like, you can schedule a brief, FREE of charge, no-obligation consultation with me at https://www.techsagesolutions.com.

About the Author

 John Hill is the CEO of TechSage Solutions, a Strategic Solutions Provider for Information Technology and Cybersecurity Services. They are also a CMMC Registered Provider Organization (RPO) focused on helping small to medium-sized Department of Defense Contractor companies prepare for their NIST SP 800-171 Self-Assessment and CMMC certification award.

Throughout his twenty-eight year military career, his years working for a DoD contractor and since starting TechSage Solutions he has focused on providing high levels of security initially as a Communications Security Specialist on Okinawa and Thailand at the end of the Vietnam War to managing the Base Network Control Center at Kelly AFB during Desert Storm to working with dozens of businesses to enhance their security. John was also instrumental in the installation of the first internet firewall at Kelly AFB and the first computer network at the Air National Guard Unit.

Over the last few years John has spoken at a number of luncheon seminars, webinars and panel discussions about cybersecurity. He was recently interviewed by Kaseya on a live podcast about the DoDs CMMC Requirements and its impact. John received a Bachelor of Science degree in Biology from the University of Texas at San Antonio in 1998. He has served on the board of directors of the San Antonio Chapter of the Armed Forces Communications and Electronics Association (AFCEA), the University of Texas at San Antonio Alumni Association, International Association of Microsoft Channel Partners and other organizations.

Made in the USA
Columbia, SC
29 January 2022

55031279R00102